A Nation On Trial: America and The War of 1812

❦ AMERICA IN CRISIS

A series of eight books on American Diplomatic History

EDITOR: *Robert A. Divine*

A Nation On Trial:

America and The War of 1812

PATRICK C. T. WHITE

University of Toronto

John Wiley & Sons, Inc., New York · London · Sydney

To the memory of my father

Preface

MORE THAN ONE HUNDRED AND FIFTY YEARS have passed since the outbreak of the War of 1812. Since that time the reason for its declaration, the conduct of its operations, and the peace which concluded it have been discussed and debated. There are, of course, some wars which are subject to a ready explanation. But the War of 1812 is not one of them. It was not fought to repel naked aggression nor was it entered on to seize territory. The issues which led to its outbreak were much more varied and complicated than that. At the root of it was America's determination to protect her honor, national interests, and sovereignty, which had been placed in jeopardy because of the long and terrible war being fought in Europe between Britain and France. In their contest for survival both powers often pursued policies that damaged American interests, but because Britain controlled the high seas her actions proved to be more immediately felt and harmful to the United States. It is no easy task for a neutral nation to protect her interests when she is caught between two great warring powers. It was doubly difficult for the United States because she had only recently won her independence, the stability of her institutions had not been tested by time or events, and her power was not great. This is why successive administrations in Washington attempted to secure relief from their distress by peaceful means. Only when every effort had failed did America turn reluctantly and hesitatingly to war.

After two years of inconclusive fighting the war was brought to an end. The Treaty of Ghent made no mention of the major issues that had played so significant a role in bringing on the conflict. Rather it simply called for a mutual restoration of oc-

cupied territory and for the creation of commissions to settle
outstanding boundary disputes. Although the War of 1812 was
of little importance to Great Britain, it had enormous significance
for the United States. By fighting it she had preserved her national honor, maintained her Republican institutions, and renewed her sense of national identity. America had, in short,
proved her capacity and determination to survive as a nation.

All students of this war are indebted to those who first examined it in detail as well as to those who have recently studied
it with a renewed sense of its importance. I am particularly grateful to Professor Robert A. Divine who invited me to write this
volume and whose perceptive criticism was of such help to me
in the preparation of the manuscript. I am indebted to William
L. Gum and his colleagues at John Wiley and Sons for their
generous editorial assistance and to Miss Freyha Hahn for her
expert typing. I should also like to thank Dr. W. Kaye Lamb,
the Dominion Archivist. All historians in Canada appreciate the
manner in which the facilities and resources of the Public Archives in Ottawa are placed at their disposal. And finally I wish
to express my gratitude to my wife whose judgment and sense
of style have been a constant aid to me. Quotations from Crown
copyright material in the Public Record Office, London, appear
by permission of the Controller of H.M. Stationery Office.

Toronto, Ontario,   PATRICK C. T. WHITE.
August 1965

Contents

MAPS

CHAPTER I

The Shadow of the Future

"IF WE SUBMIT to the pretensions of England now openly avowed," declared John C. Calhoun in 1812, "the independence of this nation is lost. . . . This is the second struggle for our liberty." [1] And to many Americans it was, for in the past decade Britain had brought heavy, and at times almost intolerable, pressure to bear upon the United States. Because of her war with Napoleon, Britain had resorted to practices that had injured America's citizens, harassed her shipping, and disrupted her economy. Further, Britain's presence in Canada and her relations with the Indians in the Northwest had convinced many Americans that she was actively engaged in fostering unrest on that long, exposed, and ill-defended frontier. For nine long years the United States had tried to moderate British policies and to secure relief from them. Everything in the arsenal of diplomacy had been used, including negotiation, economic retaliation, and the threat of war. All of them had failed. Finally, the United States became convinced that the only honorable alternative was war, and so the country reluctantly decided to take up arms.

The decision was nearly a decade in the making; when it was taken, it lacked unanimity. There were many reasons for this confusion of spirit and intent in America. It was no little thing for a newly independent nation to enter the lists against one of the two great powers in the world. There was no assurance that America would win, and there was good reason to believe that she might suffer heavy damages. Her coastline was vulner-

---

[1] *Annals of Congress*, 12th Congress, 1st Session, 1398.

1

able to attack, and it was feared that the Royal Navy would inflict severe injuries upon major ports. There was less anxiety over the prospect of invasion by land, but there was disquiet about the possibility that British-supported Indians would range along the northern boundary. A more disturbing fear concerned the ability of Republican institutions to withstand the buffeting of war. Was America strong enough internally to survive the strains that an external attack would bring? Some were so uncertain of the answer that they would have preferred not to put the nation to the test. There were also those who thought that the possibility of further negotiations had not been fully explored. They believed that incompetence in Washington had led to the existing state of affairs and that the exercise of greater diplomatic skill would save the situation. Finally, some Americans felt that the wrong enemy had been chosen. France, too, had violated the rights of the United States and should pay a price for her actions. Even Henry Clay admitted this, but he argued that Britain's aggressions were more deserving of punishment. A majority agreed with him.

The divisions of opinion in the country in 1812 reflected the complicated nature of the origins of the war itself. There had long been differences of opinion between America and Britain on many issues. Some of these disputes had been resolved by Jay's Treaty in 1794, but others, particularly the ones related to maritime disputes, had not. These grew out of the war between Britain and France. Indeed, it is not too much to say that had it not been for that struggle, there would have been no war in 1812.

Disputes over international rights are always particularly contentious. There is seldom universal agreement on what constitutes the law governing relations between nations. In the nineteenth century international law was, with few exceptions, made up of rules that had been accepted through common usage as the guidelines by which nations might conduct themselves. But custom is not permanent, and the compulsion of war could force a nation to alter the rules of the game.

This is what had frequently occurred during the years from 1803 to 1812. The most persistently baffling issue between Britain and America was impressment, and it was difficult to resolve because it touched deeply the sovereignty of both nations. The problem arose because British sailors deserted in large numbers to the American merchant marine. The war in Europe had enhanced America's position as a neutral carrier. Because her shipping increased so rapidly and because the need for crews could not be met at home, America drew upon the human resources of foreign countries. By contemporary standards, the wages she offered were high and the living conditions were excellent. To a British sailor pressed into a service that was long and dangerous and forced to work in conditions that were often appalling, shipping·under American colors could not fail to be attractive. But the drain this made upon the Royal Navy was too serious to tolerate, and so British sailors were impressed off foreign vessels.

To Americans, impressment was completely unjustifiable. But the problem was far from simple. There was, to begin with, the question of nationality. Today it is relatively easy to change citizenship, but in the nineteenth century the principle of indefeasible nationality was generally accepted. Great Britain asserted that she had the right to call upon the services of all British-born sailors when the need arose. In 1797 Lord William Grenville, the British Foreign Secretary, informed Rufus King, the American minister in London, that "the laws of Great Britain render all British sailors liable to be called upon to serve in the defence of their country . . . ." He added that "no British subject can by such a form of renunciation as that which is prescribed in the American law of naturalization divest himself of his allegiance to his sovereign." [2]

This categorical claim was emphatically denied by every American government. In 1800 John Marshall, then Secretary of State, wrote: "Those seamen who, born in a foreign country, have been adopted by this were either the subjects of Britain or some other power. The right to impress those of every other nation has not been disclaimed. Neither the one practice nor the other can be justified." Now Britain never claimed the right to impress foreign citizens from an American ship, although

---

[2] Grenville to King, March 27, 1797, *American State Papers. Class I. Foreign Relations*, II, 149.

this did happen. But she did insist upon her right to impress British subjects. It was this claim that Marshall challenged. "The case of British subjects," he said, "whether naturalized or not is more questionable, but the right even to impress them is denied." [3] The positions of the two countries were so essentially antagonistic that negotiations could not reconcile the differences.

This situation was bad enough, but what complicated it beyond the wit of man was the insistence of Britain on searching American vessels on the high seas for deserters. It was the British contention that the right to pursue fugitives extended to the limits of another nation's sovereignty. Britain did not claim the right to search American vessels within the territorial waters of the United States, nor did the United States insist that American ships could not be searched in British waters. But England did assert that she had the right to search American vessels on the high seas. The exceptions to this were the public vessels of any country. The act of stopping and searching the American frigate, the *Chesapeake*, was admittedly illegal, and Britain was quick to disavow it. But she insisted that she had the right and duty to stop and search privately owned ships. Here she ran headlong into American opposition. The United States accepted a belligerent's right to stop neutral ships on the high seas and search them for contraband, and she accepted a belligerent's right to prevent neutral vessels from entering a blockaded port. But she denied the right of any foreign power to take sailors from her ships.

The disputes over impressment and the right of search were serious enough. But what added to American anger were the abuses that so often accompanied these British practices. Although Britain did not claim the right to take American citizens, the blunt fact was that she often did while asserting that they were British. Frequently the mistake was an honest one, for similarities of language and culture made such errors possible. But sometimes a British officer whose ship was undermanned would deliberately take American sailors in order to fill out his crew. That a citizen of the Republic should lose his freedom

---

[3] Marshall to King, September 20, 1800, *ibid.*, II, 489.

on the word of one English naval officer was intolerable. James Madison spoke for his country when he said this practice was "peculiarly indefensible for it deprives the dearest rights of persons of a regular trial to which the most inconsiderable article of property, captured on the high seas, is entitled, and leaves their destiny to the will of an officer, sometimes cruel, often ignorant and generally interested, by his want of mariners, in his own decisions." Even the question of property liable to seizure, he continued, is settled before a legal tribunal. "Can it be reasonable then," he asked, "or just that a belligerent commander who is thus restricted and thus responsible in a case of mere property of trivial amount should be permitted without recurring to any tribunal whatever, to examine the crew of a neutral vessel, to decide the important question of their respective allegiance and to carry that decision into instant execution . . . ." [4] To secure the release of an American citizen from British service after his impressment was a long and difficult task. Proof of his American citizenship had to be submitted to the British Admiralty where, if it was accepted, the order for the release was granted. But, because this procedure was unsatisfactory to the United States, proofs of citizenship called "protections" were issued to her sailors. Unfortunately, these were often sold by Americans to British seamen. In Boston and other ports one could buy them for as little as a dollar. Because this was so widely known, British officers tended to dismiss their validity and impress their owners. Madison maintained, for example, that between 1797 and 1801 over 2,000 known cases of impressment took place. Certainly by 1812 well over 6,000 sailors had been taken from American ships. This practice, then, not only challenged American sovereignty but also touched the homes of thousands of American citizens. It is no wonder that it was so bitterly contested in Washington and so deeply resented throughout the land.

However, impressment and the right of search were not the only areas of serious conflict. Very nearly as important, and certainly as galling to the United States, was British interference with American trade. Of course, France, too, tried to control

---

[4] Secretary of State to Monroe, January 5, 1804, *ibid.*, II, 730.

foreign commerce. But she could do this only through the European ports that she owned or occupied, where she could use the excuse of municipal regulations to justify her actions. But Britain controlled the high seas and so could enforce her policies at will. Because of this control she was continuously and directly challenging the freedom of the United States to trade where and when she wanted.

The differences between the United States and Britain covered issues ranging from blockades to the Orders in Council. By consensus a blockade, to be legal, had to be officially declared and effective. There was no trouble over the first requirement but much over the second. It had generally been admitted that a blockade was effective if enforced by a group of ships stationed in front of a particular port and capable of preventing any ship from entering or leaving it. The condition that such a fleet had to be present at all times was qualified to allow movements necessitated by ship replacement and changes in tide and weather. The United States accepted this definition of a blockade, as did Napoleon, although he tried to obtain an even narrower one. In 1809, Napoleon's minister of foreign affairs, Champagny, informed John Armstrong, the American minister to France, that "a place is not truly blockaded until it is invested by land and sea . . . ."[5] Such a restricted interpretation was completely inadmissible to Britain. Indeed, she moved in the opposite direction when she rejected the idea of a stationary force hovering off a specific port as an essential element in a blockade. In 1806 Britain insisted upon the right to blockade an entire coast and argued that as long as it was effective, it was legal. The United States denounced this view but was unable to force Britain to make major alterations in her position.

A further clash developed over contraband. It had long been acknowledged that arms and accoutrements of war constituted contraband. But beyond this point there existed little, if any, agreement. Most writers admitted that goods other than arms might be viewed as contraband when particular conditions justified it. It was to a neutral's interest to uphold as narrow a definition of contraband as possible, just as it was to be a

---

[5] Champagny to Armstrong, August 22, 1809, *ibid.*, III, 325.

belligerent's advantage to widen the category. Britain did the latter. In 1793 British vessels were ordered to "stop and detain all ships loaded wholly or in part with Corn, Flour or Meal bound to any Port in France or any Port occupied by the armies of France . . . ." Britain justified this order by stating that all provisions were contraband when "the depriving of an enemy of these supplies is one of the means intended to be employed for reducing him to reasonable terms of peace." The United States sharply differed, asserting that the British view was "entirely new" and that neutrals were entitled to carry "the produce of their industry for exchange to all nations, belligerent or neutral as usual . . . ." [6] While the American complaint was not wholly accepted, Britain did mitigate the severity of her decrees by paying for the seized provisions. Nevertheless, the disputes over contraband remained as an irritant in the diplomatic relations between the two countries.

The problems arising from the issue of contraband and its seizure had further ramifications. One of these was the principle, advanced by America, of "free ships, free goods." It was her view that a neutral ship carrying enemy goods, other than contraband, gave to such goods the protection of the neutral flag. Hence, noncontraband French goods carried in American ships had the same "freedom" as American goods. The converse principle, "enemy ships, enemy goods," was also advanced by the United States. This was too much for Britain to tolerate. It was a principle that would rob her of the advantages of controlling the seas, for it would permit France to import her goods in neutral vessels and so circumvent any blockade. No government in London would permit this.

An equally disrupting issue was the application of the "Rule of 1756." During the eighteenth century and even later, a nation's trade with its colonies was generally a monopoly in time of peace. But during a war some powers who were weak at sea threw open their colonial commerce to neutrals so that they could continue to receive the goods that would ordinarily have been denied them. To stop this, British prize courts in

---

[6] John Bassett Moore, *International Adjudications* (6 vols., New York, 1931), IV, 14–15.

1756 condemned this trade and insisted that neutrals could not participate, during war, in a trade from which they had been excluded in time of peace. Disputes over this issue flared up after 1793 when France threw open her colonial trade to neutrals. America was quick to take advantage of this bonanza and promptly became involved in angry recriminations with Britain. Undoubtedly the "Rule of 1756" was arbitrary and novel, but Britain was not prepared to permit France to trade through the back door. And who can blame her.

Before both countries came to blows over the issue, Britain softened her stand. In January 1794, an Order in Council restricted seizures to vessels that were sailing directly from the French West Indies to Europe or attempting to enter a blockaded port in the French West Indies. In 1798, British commanders were instructed to permit neutral ships to carry goods from French colonies to their own country or to England. This opened the way for America to circumvent the Rule of 1756. American shippers could now transport goods from the French West Indies to the United States, land them, pay duty upon them, and re-export them to France or elsewhere as American goods. Legal countenance was given to this trade in the *Polly* case, which was decided in 1800. The *Polly*, an American vessel, was captured while bearing a cargo of fish, cocoa, and sugar. The cocoa and sugar had been taken on at Havana, Cuba, and shipped to America, where it had been placed in a warehouse. The customs duties had been paid, and the commodities were then re-exported to Spain. The prosecuting lawyers contended that the importation into America had not been one of true intent and had only been performed in order to transship the goods to Spain without fear of seizure. Sir William Scott, when handing down his judgment in the case, observed:

It is not my business to say what is universally the test of a *bona fide* importation. It is argued that it would not be sufficient that the duties should be paid and the cargo should be landed. If these criteria are not resorted to I should be at a loss to know what would be the tests and I am strongly disposed to hold that it would be sufficient that the goods should be landed and the duties paid.[7]

---

[7] Sir Charles Robinson (ed.), *Reports of Cases Argued and Determined in the High Court of Admiralty* (6 vols., London, 1802–1808), II, 369.

The question before the court was one of intention. Did landing goods and paying duty on them constitute bona-fide importation? If it did, then the voyage was a "broken" one, and trade between France and her colonies via the United States would be legal. If not, the voyage would be "continuous" and the cargo subject to seizure by the Royal Navy. Scott's decision made the importation bona fide, the voyage "broken," and the trade legitimate. But the decision of one court could be set aside by a higher tribunal. If the effect of the *Polly* decision was to frustrate the British blockade of Europe, one could have no doubt that Britain would find the means to upset Scott's ruling and replace it with one more favorable to her interests.

The need for this action did not become apparent until after the resumption of the European war in 1803 when the United States took every advantage of the new trade. Congress, for example, eased the burden on shippers who had to land their goods in American ports before re-export by passing an act that permitted certain goods to be reshipped immediately, with the duties on them secured by bond and drawn back with a $3\frac{1}{2}$ per cent deduction. Time was saved in other ways by American shippers who disliked the delay imposed by having to place their goods in a warehouse before re-export. Instead of landing the goods, many vessels merely touched at an American port in order to give their voyage an air of legality. It was unlikely that Britain would long recognize such voyages as "broken." In 1805 the blow fell. In the *Essex* decision of that year Sir William Grant ruled that the liberal interpretation of what constituted a "broken voyage" was no longer to be tolerated. The facts of the case were simple. An American ship, the *Essex*, had taken on a cargo of wine at Barcelona, stopped briefly in the United States, and then sailed to Havana, where it landed its wares. All this seemed straightforward enough, for the same kind of trip had been made innumerable times before without interference. But now Sir William Grant said that the *Essex* had not truly broken its voyage; that in fact the duties it had paid in America had only been nominal; and that the real intent of the ship had been to take commodities from Spain to its colonial possessions overseas. He wrote:

The mere touching at any port without importing the cargo into the common stock of the country will not alter the nature of the voyage, which continues the same in all respects; and must be considered as a voyage to the country to which the vessel is actually going for the purpose of delivering her cargo at the ultimate port.[8]

This decision did not make new law; it merely confirmed and made more stringent the upholding of the old. Nevertheless, life was made far more difficult for American shippers, for the burden of proof now lay upon them.

But worse was to follow. A large body of opinion in England wanted even harsher restrictions placed on neutral trade. Some people who advocated this did so from envy. After all, American tonnage was increasing by leaps and bounds and American shipping was competing in a trade that had once been a preserve of Britain. But others were less narrowly selfish. They simply wanted to prevent neutrals from supplying to France the materials she needed to prosecute the war. Of the pamphlets that put the case for governmental action, the most influential and cogently reasoned was "War in Disguise" by Sir James Stephen. He had been a lawyer in the West Indies and had served at the prize appeal court of the Privy Council. He was a confidant of Spencer Perceval (who later became Prime Minister) and of Sir William Scott. His arguments made a deep impression on the government. The present neutral trade, he said, carried on under the aegis of the Royal Navy, was highly damaging, for it deprived English merchants of the profits of war and destroyed the effectiveness of the blockade. Neutrals were flooding Europe with their goods. These are, he said,

. . . floated into the warehouses of our enemies, or circulated for the supply of their customers in neutral countries. They supplant or rival the British planter and merchant throughout the continent of Europe and in all the ports of the Mediterranean. They supplant even the manufacturers of Manchester, Birmingham and Yorkshire . . .

To prevent this from continuing, he insisted that the Rule of 1756 should be rigorously enforced. He stated:

If neutrals have no right, but through our own gratuitous concessions to carry on the colonial trade of our enemies, we may, after a reason-

---

[8] W. H. Phillips and A. H. Read, *Neutrality* (2 vols., New York, 1936), II, 124.

able notice withdraw the ruinous indulgence; and meantime hold those who claim the benefit of it, to a strict compliance with its terms.

He readily admitted that such a step might bring a war with these states, but such a conflict was to be preferred to a supine acquiescence in a trade that was sapping the resources of Britain and strengthening the economy of her enemies.[9] However, he did not feel that Britain would have to fight, for he was convinced that war would be too ruinous for America to contemplate. Like so many of his contemporaries, he misjudged the fiber of the Americans.

As the European war developed, the British government began to enact legislation that embodied the spirit, if not the substance, of "War in Disguise." In January 1807, England forbade neutrals to trade between ports under French control. The United States was quick to challenge the legality of this prohibition for, as a result of the French losses at Trafalgar, she was enjoying an ever larger share of the trade. The British action, Madison said, could not be justified on the grounds that a blockade was being applied for it was impossible to close off an entire coast. Nor could the order be the consequence of an alleged illegality in the trade, for if that were so, it was "an illegality which has never been applied by the British government or its Admiralty courts to an accustomed trade between ports of the same belligerent nation." The effect of this decree, Madison concluded, was unjustifiably severe. He wrote to the British Lord Chancellor, Thomas Erskine, that to deny the vessels of the United States "this legitimate and customary mode of trading with the continent of Europe . . . would be a proceeding as ruinous to our commerce as contrary to our essential rights."[10] Madison was right, but in the midst of battle international law is one of the first casualties.

Though America complained over coastal trade, she was to suffer far more from the Orders in Council and the Berlin and Milan decrees. These decrees formed the basis of the Continental system. Issued by France in November 1806, and December

---

[9] James Stephen, *War in Disguise* (London, 1805), 73.
[10] Madison to Erskine, March 29, 1807, *American State Papers, Foreign Relations*, III, 159

1807, they declared the British Isles blockaded, ordered the seizure of all British goods, and excluded from the continent, under penalty of confiscation, all ships that had first touched at a British port. Because he lacked a fleet, Napoleon could not prevent vessels from going to Britain, but, by closing the European market to her, he hoped to wreck her economy and destroy her capacity to wage war. Britain retaliated with her Orders in Council of January and November 1807, which stated that all ports excluding British ships were henceforth blockaded and that any vessel sailing to a French-controlled port without first calling at a British port would be treated as an enemy.

The position of a neutral in these circumstances was hazardous in the extreme. To sail toward France without first calling at England meant seizure by the Royal Navy; to touch at England and then sail to France meant confiscation by Napoleon. American opinion was first confused, then angered, and finally outraged. In their frustration, many wanted to declare war on both powers. But in calm reflection, if that was possible in the circumstances, it was recognized that Britain bore down more heavily upon America than did France. In 1812 it was finally decided that force, and force alone, should be used to bring relief to a distracted country.

The erosion of American rights began when Britain and France first became locked in combat in 1793. For the next eight years Britain impressed American seamen, issued Orders in Council, which adversely affected neutral trade with Europe, and enforced the odious Rule of 1756. The outraged cries of protest from the United States led to modification of some of these practices but not their abolition. America might have plunged into war over these issues had it not been for the calm restraint and cool wisdom exercised by Presidents Washington and Adams. By negotiating settlements when they could and by moderating passions when they appeared to be getting out of hand, both these administrations were able to steer clear of war.

They were helped in their task by the actions of France, for the destructive attacks by her fleets upon American commerce worked to mitigate the feelings of hostility felt toward Britain. Indeed, so angered did the United States become at the Revolutionary government in Paris that some feared war with France was inevitable. When American representatives were treated with contempt by French officials, when apologies were demanded for references that President Adams had rightly made to France, and when loans and tributes were asked of the United States before peaceful negotiations could be undertaken, the intensity of anti-French feeling reached the flash point. But the calmness that had been used when dealing with Britain was also employed when treating with France. As a result, the United States disengaged herself from the Franco-American treaties of 1778 and continued to pursue a policy of neutrality toward the belligerent powers in Europe. She protested against abuses of her rights, she took action to preserve her interests, but she avoided war. When the Peace of Amiens ended the European struggle in 1801, a sense of relief swept through America. The Anglo-French war had created the majority of the disputes that had threatened to entangle the United States with the two great world powers. Now that these nations had come to terms the contentious issues, which had so distressed Washington, disappeared. But unfortunately for the United States, the peace reached at the turn of the century was to be only an interlude, and a short one at that, in a greater struggle. Less than two years after it was reached, it was broken, and the war between Britain and France was renewed with savage vigor. Both powers extended the area of struggle; now that it had become a battle for survival, they treated neutrals in a much more cavalier fashion than before. When one is fighting for one's life, one is not much concerned if innocent bystanders are hurt in the fray.

President Jefferson recognized that the war in Europe would bring grave danger to America. Indeed, his skill was to be put to a severe and continuous testing until he left office. The situations that he faced called for diplomatic foresight, cool deliberation, and the determination to use military power if necessary. Although these elements were not wholly lacking in him, neither were they present in sufficient force. The President himself viewed war with a troubled conscience, for he believed that rational men can sit down and resolve differences without resorting to brute strength. But he also recognized that all men do not act reasonably, and that, as a consequence, to compromise forever in the face of danger would invite disaster. He once said that, "Peace . . . has been our principle, peace is our interest . . .," [11] but he also admitted that, if America were not respected abroad, she would become the "plunder of all nations." [12] He defended American rights with a legalistic passion and upheld international law to a point near pedantry, but often his interpretations of it were no more justified than those of his hated antagonist, George Canning. His approach to diplomacy was a mixture of the ideal and the practical, for he could be stubborn in defense of what he deemed right but shift course when he decided that his cause was hopeless. His actions often irritated his friends and puzzled his enemies. Yet it must always be recognized that his range of choice was narrow, and the means of implementing his goals were limited. He had neither the power nor the position to force his will upon others, and if he appeared to act without consistency, the explanation was as often to be found in the complexities of external circumstances as it was in the nature of his own personality.

It is one of the ironies of history that Jefferson's greatest diplomatic triumph contributed in some fashion to the coming of the war that he so earnestly sought to avoid. When he secured the Louisiana Territory in 1803, he not only freed America from French pressure but also made it unnecessary for his country to maintain close ties with Britain. In 1802 he had written to Robert R. Livingston, the minister to France, "the day that France takes possession of N. Orleans fixes the sentence which is to restrain her forever within her low water mark." He added "From that moment we must marry ourselves

---

[11] Jefferson to Kosciuszko, April 13, 1811, A. A. Lipscomb and A. E. Bergh (eds.), *The Writings of Thomas Jefferson* (20 vols., Library Edition, Washington, 1903), XIII, 41–42.

[12] Jefferson to Thomas Cooper, February 8, 1806, Jefferson Mss, quoted Perkins, *Prologue to War*, 41.

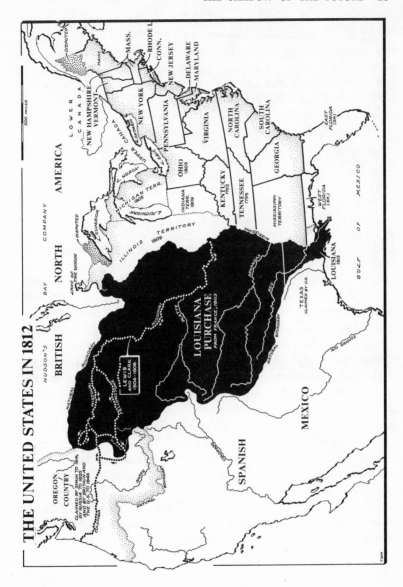

THE UNITED STATES IN 1812

to the British fleet and nation." [13] Napoleon's unexpected decision to rid himself of the entire Louisiana Territory saved Jefferson from a projected alliance with Britain.

But the acquisition of this enormous area led to complications that no one had anticipated. The transfer of the territory gave a new sense of power to the United States. Sir Edward Thornton, the British chargé d'affaires in Washington, had once been warmly cultivated there, but he now wrote:

. . . a real change has taken place . . . which may be dated from the first arrival of the Intelligence relative to the Louisiana Purchase and which has since derived additional Force and Acrimony from the opinion that Great Britain cannot resist under her present Pressure the new claims of the United States . . . . [14]

It is true that some in New England opposed the bargain, but even John Quincy Adams admitted that American power and security had been vastly enhanced by the President's action.

In addition, the purchase from France of Louisiana destroyed a convention that had been carefully negotiated with Britain and that would have removed a series of abrasive boundary disputes between British North America and the United States. These had their origin in the Treaty of 1783 and ran from Passamaquoddy Bay in the east to the Mississippi River in the west. The convention, signed in London after the negotiations had been completed with Napoleon, came to the Senate floor in October 1803. But, save for some members from the Northeast, the Senate insisted on removing from the agreement Article V which dealt with the boundary from the Lake of the Woods to the Mississippi River. The Louisiana Purchase, it was argued, gave the United States rights in the area, which were as yet undetermined, and it would be foolhardy to sign them away. The British government could have accepted the modified convention and perhaps should have, for the removal of any

---

[13] Jefferson to Livingston, April 18, 1802, Paul L. Ford (ed.), *The Writings of Thomas Jefferson* (10 vols., New York, 1892–1899), VIII, 145.

[14] Thornton to Hammond, January 24, 1804, quoted A. Steel, "Anthony Merry and the Anglo-American Dispute about Impressment," *Cambridge Historical Journal*, IX, 3, 1949, 338.

dispute with the United States would have served her interests. But she preferred to reject the whole rather than preserve any of its parts.

Finally, the Louisiana Purchase played, in the eyes of some, a role in Jefferson's determination to end impressment. Thornton wrote in 1804 that "in the question of Impressment, he has hit precisely the only point by which at present he could gain the northern states; for though they suffer comparatively little from its pretended Greevence [sic], it has always been a Subject of great and bitter Complaint." [15] But Thornton misjudged the President. It is doubtful that Jefferson was prepared to play politics with such an explosive issue, for the consequences of a British rebuff might have been the unleashing of forces that he would be unable to control. It is far more likely that the President rightly recognized impressment as an issue that had to be settled if Anglo-American relations were not to be placed in serious jeopardy. Rufus King, the American minister in London, was quick to recognize this in 1803. When he saw that war was "inevitable" between Britain and France, he hastily opened talks on impressment.[16] The day after he signed the boundary convention he held a conference with Lord St. Vincent on the subject. Here he argued that the advantages Britain gained from the practice were far outweighed by the "irritation and bad humor" that it created in the United States.[17] After an exchange of views, King drew up a convention that would have abolished impressment on the "high seas and without the jurisdiction of either party" for a period of five years.[18] Lord St. Vincent consulted with Lord Hawkesbury, the Foreign Secretary, and then proposed an alteration in the draft so that the "narrow seas," that is, those waters surrounding the British Isles, would have been excluded from the treaty. This change was required, the British said, because these waters have been "immemorially considered within the dominions of Great

---

[15] *Ibid.*, 338.
[16] King to the Secretary of State, no. 85, March 17, 1803, C. R. King, *The Life and Correspondence of Rufus King* (6 vols., New York, 1898), IV, 229.
[17] *Ibid.*, IV, 256.
[18] King to the Secretary of State, July 1803, *American State Papers, Foreign Relations*, II, 503.

Britain." [19] King could not accept this qualification, for it would have meant the acceptance of the principle of impressment, even though the area of its exercise would have been vastly reduced.

Shortly after the news of King's failure reached America, Jefferson proposed that a fresh effort be made to resolve the dispute. He suggested to Madison that perhaps Britain and the United States could agree to act upon the proposals put forward by King without writing them into a formal treaty. Madison then wrote James Monroe, who had replaced King in London, suggesting that the Royal Navy immediately desist from impressing on the high seas and warning that, if it did not, its actions would "overcome the calculating policy of the present Executive and provoke the public temper into an irresistible impetus on the public councils." [20] That it did not do so was attributable to two things. The first was that impressment in the last few months of 1803 did not reach the outrageous proportions which were to characterize it later. The second was that Jefferson earnestly wished an accommodation with Britain, and both he and his ministers were certain that the cabinet in London would prove to be reasonable and sympathetic. Madison wrote that "the present administration in Great Britain appears more liberal and cordial towards the United States than any preceding one." [21]

Given this atmosphere, the administration decided to strive for more than an informal understanding. Instead, Madison instructed Monroe to secure a settlement of the major maritime differences that the European war had again brought forward. The demands that the American minister was to make were many, the concessions that he was instructed to offer were few. A settlement was required of impressment, blockades, visiting and searching on the high seas, contraband, and trade with hostile colonies. In return for concessions on these subjects, the United States was ready to agree to a mutual return of

---

[19] *Ibid.*, 504.

[20] Madison to Monroe, October 10, 1803, Gaillard Hunt, *The Writings of James Madison* (7 vols., New York, 1900–1910), VII, 201.

[21] Madison to Monroe, March 8, 1804, *Letters and Other Writings of James Madison* (4 vols., New York, 1865), II, 201.

deserters and a ban on the export of contraband to enemy territory. Under the most favorable circumstances and in the fairest diplomatic weather, the United States would have been fortunate to have secured a tenth of what she wanted. In the rough political climate of Europe in 1804, it was little wonder that Monroe found the negotiations so difficult to conduct and an agreement so hard to reach.

The American minister opened talks with a government led by Henry Addington. Addington's weaknesses and vacillations had encouraged Washington to think that he would be an easy mark. After all, the diarist Thomas Creevey had described the Prime Minister as "the feeblest—lowest almost—of Men, still more so of Ministers." [22] But, dilatory and incompetent as Addington was, he did not wish to end policies vital to the security of the nation, nor would his country permit him to do so. As these included all the maritime practices on which Monroe was authorized to negotiate, it is easy to see how difficult his task was. But his job was also complicated by the fact that Addington held office for only a brief period. He had occupied his post on the sufferance of William Pitt, and when the latter tired of his inadequacies, he and his followers drove him from the government. The new administration was a formidable one led by Pitt himself. Pitt had once been a friend of America and had even supported liberalizing trade with her. But that day had passed, and now he was consumed with the desire to destroy Napoleon. As Creevey said, Pitt was "all for war, and for war without end." [23] To achieve this he was prepared to use every military and economic measure at hand and not count the cost. The pace of impressment was accelerated, and its practice was exercised in a manner particularly galling to the United States. Throughout the summer and autumn of 1804, for example, the British frigate H.M.S. *Leander* lay off the port of New York and impressed sailors from ships that entered and left that harbor. What was done in sight of American shores was repeated one hundredfold on the high seas. Indeed, between 1803 and 1806, more sailors were seized

---

[22] Sir Robert Maxwell (ed.), *The Creevey Papers* (London, 1903), 19.
[23] *Ibid.*, 15.

from American ships than in the years between 1795 and 1801. It is little wonder that the United States began to feel that it had won the war for independence but was fast losing the fruits of that victory.

It was no surprise, then, when Monroe found that he could make no progress with this hard and unyielding administration. By the autumn of 1804 he was so disheartened that he toyed with the idea of terminating all talks. But he decided merely to suspend them while he went to Spain to fulfill another mission. If he had hoped that conditions would improve in the interim, he was sadly disillusioned. At home, public opinion was rapidly becoming aroused. Congress passed an act authorizing the President to interdict American ports to armed vessels of foreign nations and to arrest and indict foreign officers who came within American jurisdiction after committing on the high seas "any trespass or tort or any spoliation on board any vessel of the United States . . . ."[24] And this act, Madison took pleasure in informing Anthony Merry, the British minister in Washington, covered "the impressment of British subjects as well as others . . . ."[25] Then, in the summer of 1805, came the *Essex* decision, which was zealously enforced by the Royal Navy. Scores of American ships were seized and their officers hauled into Admiralty courts. Fortunately the law officers of the Crown tempered the enthusiasm of the Royal Navy, and many of the ships were released. But the damage was done, for America reacted violently to what was deemed to be highhanded and arbitrary treatment. As a result of this new crisis in Anglo-American relations, Monroe hastened to reopen discussions with the British government. But these talks proved to be as fruitless and barren as the preceding ones. Monroe finally concluded that Britain had no intention of reaching a settlement, but rather that her envy of American prosperity was driving her to "subject our commerce at present and hereafter to every restraint in their power." If the United States did not resist,

---

[24] Henry Adams, *History of the United States during the Administrations of Jefferson and Madison* (9 vols., New York, 1889–1891), II, 397.
[25] Madison to Monroe, March 6, 1805, *American State Papers, Foreign Relations*, III, 107.

doing so. Grenville was determined to pursue the
France with every means at hand, and so he was
reat America with sympathy or consideration. Even
was tired, old, and sick, and while he had once
principle of American liberty, he was neither able
to do so now. It was England's life that was at stake
's security that was being threatened. If the price of
riendship would lead to the weakening of Britain's
x would not pay it.

ime was running out. In February 1806, the ministry
Talents" was in office, but by April Fox was so ill,
use of the duties he had assumed, that he was warned
himself from the House of Commons. In June his
und his condition incurable; by the middle of
he was dead. America's illusion of better times did
th him, but the stormy course of events during his
d in office should have given warning of the difficult
d.

the instability inherent in the ministry, it decided that
hould be given to American complaints and that some
sture of good will might be made to her. The degree
an irritation over British practices was now far too
be totally ignored. Senator Robert Wright of Mary-
example, had introduced a bill in Congress in January
ich would have classified impressment as piracy, and
s severe measure was shelved, less stringent ones
ollowed. Representative Andrew Gregg asked Congress
consideration to a bill that would have excluded all
oods from the country. A more modest measure, how-
s proposed, one which would have restricted Gregg's
at only those British goods would be barred for which
es could not be found elsewhere. This last device found
ith both Congress and the administration—with Con-
ecause it would end the frustrations members were
over administrative inaction, and with the administration
it would punish Britain by means short of war. Indeed,
n found the measure particularly attractive because it
permit him to eschew the use of physical force, which he
and because it would provide the only kind of pressure

worse indignities would follow; if she stood fast, England's "whole system of conduct toward the United States would change." [26]

This was brave advice, but its implementation required a firmness from Washington that was not present. Far from wanting this kind of direct confrontation with Britain, Jefferson was now entertaining the idea of an alliance with her. The stakes for which Jefferson was playing would have to be high in order to justify such a step. And high they were, for the President was hoping to gain Spanish territory east of the Mississippi River. For some time he had been casting covetous eyes upon West Florida and trying diligently to gain satisfaction from Spain for the seizure of American vessels in Spanish waters after 1796. Monroe had left London for Madrid in 1804 with instructions to obtain a settlement in these matters. His mission was a failure partly because Spain was not at war with Britain, and the support that she now enjoyed from France gave her sufficient confidence to reject American overtures. This turn in events strengthened Jefferson's idea of an alliance with Britain, and he broached the idea to Madison. He confided to his Secretary of State his conviction that France was now actively hostile toward America and that, to preserve his country's security, it was necessary to secure closer and more intimate ties with Britain. However, both Madison and Albert Gallatin, Secretary of the Treasury, warned him to pursue this goal with great caution and pointed out the pitfalls that lay in his path. Britain would want services rendered in return for an alliance, and the cost of these might be uncomfortably steep.

Circumstances overseas, rather than the innate caution of Gallatin or the studied judgment of Madison, caused Jefferson to shelve the idea. First came the news of the *Essex* decision and the seizures that followed it. Then came the reports of the extension of the war in Europe, when Austria and Russia joined with Britain to oppose Napoleon. The war in Europe would not permit the United States to act with leisure and secure through negotiation what she had previously felt could only be got by coercion. The extension of war in Europe gave relief to Jefferson

[26] Monroe to Madison, October 18, 1805, *ibid.*, 107.

over the problem of Florida. But unhappily it brought greater burdens over neutral rights. For Napoleon's victory at Austerlitz gave him control of Europe, and Nelson's triumph at Trafalgar gave Britain supremacy on the ocean. The nature of these two events shaped the strategy of these two great powers, and their strategy in turn slowly and inexorably ground away at American rights.

CHAPTER II

The Failure of Negot

IF JEFFERSON FAILED to grasp
bound to flow from events
by the death of Pitt. The P
weight of office at home and
died in 1806. A false but wi
over America, for it was belie
might be led by Charles Jame
work swiftly to heal the breac
The conviction that Fox would
ment was realized, but the exp
course of events was not.

The reasons for this were th
headed by Lord Grenville, not
Secretary. It was asking too mu
old antagonist like Fox to form
pared to "swallow the bitter pill"
ministry. This new administration
Grenville, Fox, Addington, now L
porters. And it was an uncertain
hold office held it together as n
Further, the opposition to it of t
formidable. A coalition governme
England, and a weak coalition had l
the beginning the new administr
difficulties and unlikely to prove its
free hand toward the United States.

In the second place, even had this
ease tensions with America, circums

vent it from
war against
unlikely to
worse, Fox
defended th
nor willing
and Englan
American
position, Fo
Finally,
of "All the
partly beca
to absent
doctors fo
September
not die wi
short peric
times ahea
Despite
a hearing
modest ge
of Ameri
intense to
land, for
1806, wh
while th
quickly f
to give
British g
ever, wa
bill so th
substitu
favor w
gress b
feeling
because
Jefferso
would
loathed

available to a country weak in military and naval power.

As the process of negotiating had not yet been exhausted, the measure—though passed in April 1806—was not put into force immediately. Rather it was held in the background—until September 1807, in fact—while Monroe and William Pinkney pressed America's case in London. The prospects, Jefferson felt, were bright, and he wrote:

With England I flatter myself our difficulties will be dissipated by the disaster of her allies, the change of her ministry, and the measures which Congress are likely to adopt to furnish motives for her becoming just to us: and on the whole I cannot but hope that in the general settlement of affairs of nations now on the tapis, ours also will be satisfactorily settled; so as to ensure us those years of peace & prosperity which will place us beyond the reach of European wrong-doers.[1]

The President was not wholly wrong in his assessment of the situation, for it seemed to be improving. Parliament, after a protracted and sometimes bitter debate, had passed an Intercourse Bill, which allowed neutral vessels to conduct a limited trade with the West Indies. Coincidentally with this, Anthony Merry was replaced by David Erskine as British minister in Washington.

Merry's tenure in the American capital had not been a happy one. Washington had never been considered the most attractive city for a posting. Charles Bagot, writing in 1816, had said that after his first three months there he had "got over most of my first disagreeables. . . ." He reported: "They [Americans] are not worse than I expected—but they are not better. From democracy and grossness under the titles of liberty and simplicity Good Lord deliver us." [2] Merry, who unlike Bagot was rigid, pompous, and without imagination or humor, did not find life in America disagreeable—he found it downright horrifying. It was difficult for him to find satisfactory housing and acceptable food, and his first impression of the city led him to cry out, "So miserable is our Situation." Physical discomfort might be accepted in the

---

[1] Jefferson to Paine, March 25, 1806, Paul L. Ford (ed.), *The Writings of Thomas Jefferson* (10 vols., New York, 1892–1899), XI, 248.

[2] Bagot to Huskisson, private, July 4, 1816. Huskisson Papers, Add. MSS 38741.

loyal service of one's country, but the lack of manners he found too much to bear. When he presented his credentials to the President, the chief executive greeted him informally in shabby clothes and down-at-the-heel slippers. When he attended a formal dinner at the White House, he had had to conduct, with his formidable wife, a swift foot race to secure a place at the table. A later dinner at Madison's reinforced his first impressions. The assembly was made up of the secretaries of departments and their wives. The secretaries, Merry asserted, were a "Set of Beings as little without the Manner as without the appearance of Gentlemen." This lack of respectable company was "so degrading" and "so personally disagreeable" as to have "become almost intolerable." It was all so appalling that he wrote, "Every thing else in the federal city is equally as perfectly savage." [3]

It was little wonder then that Merry was ill at ease in Washington and found it difficult to appreciate or understand the United States and its aspirations. His recall to London (on the spurious but familiar grounds of ill-health) was essential to an Anglo-American rapprochement. His successor, David Erskine, was young and inexperienced, but he did have certain advantages. He did not approach America as a vast uncharted wilderness populated by half-civilized savages, for his wife was the daughter of a distinguished member of Philadelphia society. He was, further, the son of the current Chancellor of the Exchequer, and so had close ties with the cabinet. Because of these factors his appointment was welcomed in Washington as a sign of a renewed British interest in conciliation.

How far the signs of friendship could be translated into a reality was to be tested by Monroe and Pinkney in London. Both the American negotiators approached their task with cautious enthusiasm. Monroe had experienced long delays and frustrations in his earlier efforts there, but the dual mission appeared to hold out more chance of success. However, the demands that the American team was instructed to make were stiff, and it soon became clear, as it had in the past, that diplomatic skill would not prove sufficiently powerful to overcome the national interests of Britain.

---

[3] Merry to Hammond, private, December 7, 1803, F.O. 5:41.

The instructions that Madison gave to Monroe and Pinkney called on them to secure the abolition of impressment and a modification of what constituted contraband. The Secretary of State really wished to see contraband eliminated entirely, but, knowing that this was a hopeless proposition, he suggested that foodstuffs and naval supplies should not be subject to seizure. He preferred to see the doctrine of "free ships—free goods" upheld but was prepared to surrender the principle, if Britain would open up trade with neutral colonies which was prohibited under the Rule of 1756. He also wanted indemnity for damages inflicted upon American ships by vessels of the Royal Navy, but he was not prepared to take a strong stand on the issue of blockades. As he observed, Britain had ceased blockading the entire French West Indies and was confining blockades to specified ports. Finally, Madison proposed that "all armed belligerent ships should be expressly and effectually restrained from making seizures and searches within a certain distance from our coasts, or taking station near our harbors commodious for these purposes." [4] The need for this proposal arose from the actions of the British frigate *Leander*, which had, in the course of activities off the port of New York, opened fire on an American ship and killed one of the crew. The public outcry and near-riot following this regrettable incident convinced Madison of the necessity of ending this practice. Repetition of acts of this nature could only widen the gulf between Britain and America and push them toward a war which neither wanted.

Of all the articles proposed by Madison, only two were indispensable in his view. They were the ones on impressment and neutral trade with belligerent colonies. Before Pinkney arrived in London, this indispensable minimum was reduced to one, for Fox informed Monroe of a blockade from Brest to the Elbe, which contained a loophole permitting American vessels to circumvent the Rule of 1756. This loophole was the provision that made the blockade absolute only in the stretch of coast from the Seine to Ostend. Outside of these limits neutral ships could trade with Europe in goods that were neither enemy prop-

---

[4] Madison to Monroe and Pinkney, May 17, 1806, *American State Papers. Class I. Foreign Relations*, III, 166–173.

erty nor contraband. As an effort was already being made to prohibit trade in goods from the United States that might have originated in enemy colonies, the way was open to avoid, partly or wholly, the Rule of 1756. When Pinkney arrived in London, therefore, he and Monroe had only to secure a settlement of impressment. Unfortunately, they might just as well have tried to steal the crown jewels.

In June 1806, the Americans were ready to begin their task, but Fox's grave illness prevented him from having discussions with them. Preferring not to negotiate with subordinates, the American diplomats delayed discussions, but when it became clear that the Foreign Secretary's health was not improving, they broached their demands to Lord Grenville. The difficulty of their task was immediately made apparent to them when he said that a settlement of impressment would be extraordinarily hard to secure. It was imperative, he insisted, that Britain maintain this practice, for England had to avail herself of the services of her seamen in times of war. So long as the government clung to this view, the problem would prove to be intractable.

Shortly after this initial meeting, however, the government nominated Lords Holland and Auckland to treat with Monroe and Pinkney. On August 27 serious negotiations began. The two British representatives were open to persuasion. Holland was a nephew of Fox and although he was young and inexperienced, he was sympathetic toward the United States. Auckland was an older and more seasoned campaigner, but he, too, earnestly wanted to see a rapprochement with America. Monroe and Pinkney made their minimum demands—the abolition of impressment on the high seas and in ports (although it was clear they would not insist upon the latter), and the restoration of the principle of the "broken voyage" as it had been construed before the *Essex* decision. Both the British representatives understood without equivocation that the American position was absolutely firm on the question of impressment on the high seas. They hoped, however, that the Americans might accept the practice in the English Channel as well as in British ports. But this was an uncertain possibility, for it must be remembered that King had broken off negotiations in 1803 over the issue of impressment in the "narrow seas"—although at that time the phrase admittedly encompassed all the waters surrounding the British Isles. Holland and Auckland did feel fairly certain that in order to secure a settlement on impressment, Monroe and Pinkney might make some concessions on trade. As Holland said, "unless they misrepresent things in America, they would willingly yield a point on the latter to obtain anything from us on the former." [5]

Although the British negotiators were apparently desirous of securing an agreement on this most difficult of all issues, they also realized how complicated it was, for two national interests were in conflict. They were reluctant, they said, to surrender the right of search and impressment on the high seas lest American ships become "receptacles for deserters to any amount. . . ." [6] On the other hand, they admitted that it was incumbent upon the United States to "protect their citizens from being compelled to fight the battles of a foreign power." [7] They suggested to the cabinet, therefore, that Britain might give up the right of impressment on the high seas for a short period. In return, the United States would not only use its courts to aid in the returning of British seamen but would also permit British ships to stop and search American vessels on the high seas for them. The captain of any ship could, when faced with this kind of search, either turn over to the boarding party any alleged British seaman or provide satisfactory proof that he was not a British subject. This might have been a solution to the problem, but it bristled with difficulties. In the first place, it continued the right of visit and search, which the Americans had consistently opposed and which, at a later date, was to be responsible for their refusal to enter into a treaty designed to end the slave trade. In the second place, it did not come to grips with the problem of binational seamen. Britain, with her belief in indefeasible nationality, could and would continue to impress British-born but American-

---

[5] William W. Grenville, *The Manuscripts of J. B. Fortescue, Esq.* (preserved at Dropmore, Royal Historical Manuscript Commission, 10 vols., London, 1892–1927), VIII, 310.

[6] Monroe and Pinkney to Madison, September 11, 1806, *American State Papers, Foreign Relations*, III, 133.

[7] Holland and Auckland to Howick, October 20, 1806, F.O. 5:51, quoted Anthony Steel, "Impressment in the Monroe-Pinkney Negotiation, 1806–1807," *American Historical Review*, LVII (January, 1952), 357.

naturalized citizens. As King wrote, "That allegiance is unalienable and seamen liable to impressment are two points upon which English lawyers and Statesmen entertain no doubt. . . ." Of course, the moment an American seaman of British origin was forcibly taken, the whole issue of impressment would explode again with renewed anger and bitterness.

Yet, despite these difficulties, the British negotiators were offering a substantial concession. To suggest the ending of impressment, even for a limited time and even with the proposed conditions, was a mark of Holland's and Auckland's earnest desire to reach a settlement with America. In their judgment a concession of this magnitude was absolutely necessary, for without it no reconciliation with the United States was possible. The reception their proposals received from Monroe and Pinkney convinced them that a final agreement could be achieved, and further discussions were held to hammer out the details. In these talks the Americans made a number of concessions. They agreed to a stipulation that would call for Congress to enact a law to make it a penal offense for commanders of American vessels to accept deserters from Britain. They also agreed to extend the definition of deserters so that it would include "seafaring people quitting their (Britain's) service." They could hardly have gone further in being reasonable and responsible.

It was now the turn of Holland and Auckland to show their good faith. They submitted the articles to the cabinet for approval. But before the government made a decision, it asked the opinion of the Admiralty and certain law officers of the Crown. Unfortunately for all concerned, these gentlemen had grave doubts about the wisdom of the projected agreement. They informed the cabinet that it was the King's prerogative to require the services of "all his seafaring subjects." Further, it was his prerogative to seize them by force in any area not within the territorial limits of another power. They declared that, because the high seas were extraterritorial, the merchant vessels of other powers navigating there were not admitted to possess "such a jurisdiction as to protect British subjects from the exercise of the King's prerogative over them." [8]

---

[8] Monroe and Pinkney to Madison, November 11, 1806, *American State Papers, Foreign Relations*, III, 138.

These views on impressment gave support to the position on the subject held by many members of the government, including that of the Foreign Secretary. As a result, the cabinet decided that even a modified surrender of the practice should not be contemplated. Instead, a counterproject was presented to the Americans. They rejected it on the grounds that its pretensions were inadmissible, but they also continued to argue long and earnestly for an accommodation on impressment. Holland and Auckland recognized and sympathized with the dilemma of the Americans. Indeed, Auckland went so far as to urge his government to bend a little. Even a hint of reconciliation, he pleaded, would be of advantage to Britain. But the cabinet remained adamant and refused to offer any concessions to Monroe and Pinkney.

The only question remaining was whether negotiations should continue on the other articles of the proposed convention. Monroe and Pinkney were only too aware that their instructions ordered them to secure a settlement of impressment and that any agreement failing to do this would be totally unacceptable to Jefferson. But at the same time they feared the consequences that might follow the abrupt termination of their talks. Holland and Auckland urged them to remain and complete a treaty that would, by removing the differences over other matters, be a means of "drawing close the ties of connexion between the two countries." The British representatives also put it on record that the greatest caution would be observed in the impressment of British seamen and the greatest care taken to protect American citizens from any molestation or injury. They concluded their representations with the cogent argument that, as there had been few recent complaints over impressment, "no inconvenience can result from the postponement of an article subject to so many difficulties." [9]

After due consideration of all the factors involved, Monroe and Pinkney decided that they could best serve the interests of their country by acceding to the British request, for they were convinced that a partial agreement was better than none at all. Before they did this they took care to inform the British that

---

[9] Holland and Auckland to Monroe and Pinkney, November 8, 1806, *ibid.*, III, 140.

their government would not feel bound to accept such a treaty, for their instructions had categorically demanded a settlement of impressment. Having done this they then comforted themselves with the thought that, without retreating a single step from their government's position on impressment, they had secured a solemn pledge that Britain would so regulate the practice that no injury would be inflicted upon American citizens. The binding character of that promise, resting as it did upon the pledged word of the British government, convinced them that the protection offered to their countrymen justified their acceptance of the British invitation to continue negotiations on the other articles of the proposed convention.

The decision taken by Monroe and Pinkney has been the subject of continuing controversy. They have been condemned by many for violating their instructions, and they have been criticized by some for weakening under British pressure. For surrendering on impressment, they have been charged with departing from the principles of the President and placing commercial considerations on a higher plane than national pride or honor. Britain, too, has not been free from criticism; she has been denounced for rejecting the opportunity to remove the greatest source of friction with the United States and for casting away the chance to secure American friendship when it would have aided her in the war with France. Much of this criticism is valid, but Monroe's and Pinkney's position was enormously difficult. In 1810 Monroe, looking back at the dilemma he faced, expressed the conviction that he had acted wisely. Britain was not then, he said,

... willing to yield any portion of what she called her maritime rights, under the light pressure of the non-importation law, to a power which had no maritime force, not even sufficient to protect any one of its ports against a small squadron and which had so recently submitted to great injuries and indignities from powers that had not a ship at sea. Under such circumstances it seemed to me to be highly for the interests of our country, and to the credit of our government to get out of the general scrape as best we could, and with the great maritime power on what might be called fair and reasonable conditions if such could be obtained. . . . The treaty was an honourable and advantageous adjustment with England. . . . Had Mr. Jefferson accepted that Treaty he would, in my opinion, have afforded ample protection to our commerce and seamen against England, who has such vast means of annoying them.[10]

Monroe really struck at the heart of the matter. National honor can only be upheld by power; without it compromise has to be resorted to and humiliation risked. Pride is a luxury for the weak, whereas firmness and inflexibility are the prerogatives of the strong. What America can insist upon in the middle of the twentieth century, Britain could demand in her era of power and majesty.

Once Monroe and Pinkney had made the decision to continue negotiations on the remaining issues, a swift agreement was reached. On December 31, 1806, a treaty was signed that secured a settlement of almost every outstanding dispute between Great Britain and the United States. It covered a number of subjects, of which the two most important were contraband and neutral trade with a belligerent's colonies. Contraband was to be limited to a designated list of articles, which included arms and accoutrements of war but not provisions. American trade between Europe and "enemy" colonies was to be permitted, subject to certain regulations. First, a neutral could not trade with a blockaded port. Second, the goods either from Europe or from a belligerent's colonies had to be landed in the United States where duties were to be paid before they could be exported to their particular destination. Upon re-exportation and after drawback, they were to pay a duty of one per cent of the value. Goods from colonies imported into the United States were to have the accustomed import duties paid, and upon re-exportation were to be subject after drawback to a two per cent duty on the value. This gave the United States what it wanted—the restoration of trade conditions to the halcyon days following the *Polly* case when American commerce had flourished so vigorously.

With the treaty completed and the commissioners ready to sign, Monroe and Pinkney appeared at last to have completed their task. But nothing had been easy for them; before they could set their signatures to the documents, events in Europe played them false and placed the whole settlement in jeopardy

---

[10] Monroe to Taylor, September 10, 1810, S. M. Hamilton (ed.), *The Writings of James Monroe* (7 vols., New York, 1898–1903), V, 130.

again. On November 21, 1806, Napoleon issued the Berlin Decree declaring a blockade of the British Isles and ordering that all British manufactures and colonial produce be considered lawful prize. When the news first arrived in England, governmental concern was so great that Monroe and Pinkney feared negotiations would be long delayed, if not completely suspended. Certainly Holland and Auckland were aware that the Berlin Decrees might force England to retaliate against France, and they were reluctant to sign a treaty that would limit the choice of weapons their country might wish to use in countering Napoleon's extraordinary measures. A revival of the Rule of 1756 might, for example, be necessary. However, Monroe and Pinkney prevailed upon the British to sign the treaty, but a price was exacted. In a formal note to the Americans, Lords Holland and Auckland insisted that, in the event Napoleon persisted in applying the Berlin Decrees, either the United States would guarantee that she would not "submit to such innovations," or His Majesty would not consider himself "bound by the signature of his commissioners to ratify the treaty; or precluded from adopting such measures as may seem necessary for counteracting the designs of his enemy." [11]

On March 3, 1807, Erskine, the British minister in Washington, received the treaty and immediately rushed to Madison with it. His haste stemmed from the fact that the Senate session ended that day, and he hoped that the President would detain Congress in order to have the treaty promptly ratified. He need not have so exercised himself, for Madison and Jefferson were neither prepared to approve the treaty nor to submit it to the Senate for ratification. As Madison said, it would have been impossible to secure Senate approval unless the issue of impressment was settled. As for the qualifying clause added at the last moment, that in itself "would have prevented . . . the ratification of the treaty." [12] Jefferson's position was equally firm. He had earlier conveyed to Monroe and Pinkney his opinion that, if no stipulation on impressment could be secured

---

[11] Holland and Auckland to Monroe and Pinkney, December 31, 1806, *American State Papers, Foreign Relations*, III, 152.

[12] Erskine to Howick, No. 8, March 6, 1807, F.O. 5:52.

in London, it would be better to end negotiations without any formal agreement. Nothing would persuade him to alter this view. When Erskine saw him on March 6, he was told that impressment was a *sine qua non* of the treaty and that no administration, however popular, could secure ratification of a treaty with the qualifications that the British ministry had added. Erskine left this meeting convinced that, if the impressment question could be resolved, the treaty would be heartily welcomed; but without an article on that subject he doubted whether the present administration, or any future one for that matter, would dare conclude a settlement. Four days later he sent the disappointing news to England that the President was returning the treaty unratified. In taking this step, Erskine said, Jefferson was supported by public opinion. Indeed, Madison later wrote to Monroe that the President felt it desirable to establish harmony between Britain and America and that he wished him to continue his efforts to secure the abolition of impressment. It was, of course, a vain and useless hope, but as long as the practice continued, the need for negotiation remained.

Jefferson's decision to reject the treaty out of hand has caused as much controversy as Monroe's and Pinkney's determination to continue negotiations without first resolving the issue of impressment. Some have suggested that Jefferson was never serious in his desire to end impressment and that he simply used it as an instrument of policy. As long as Napoleon was in power, it has been argued, "a state of neither peace nor war with Britain was in his [Jefferson's] judgment a clear American interest and the impressment controversy, properly exploited, was a useful means to that end." [13] Timothy Pickering, a staunch Federalist and a bitter opponent of the President, was certainly convinced that this was Jefferson's position. Mr. Jefferson, he wrote,

... *has determined not to enter into any treaty of amity and commerce with Great Britain.* . . . *I do not believe that his attempts have been sincere. And therefore he has made and insisted upon concessions*

---

[13] Anthony Steel, "Impressment in the Monroe-Pinkney Negotiation, 1806–1807," *American Historical Review*, LVII (January, 1952), 369.

which he was morally certain Great Britain would not yield: Such as the absolute protection of all seamen sailing under the flag, in all our merchant vessels; and the free carrying trade on the coasts and between the mother countries and colonies of her enemies. Could he have obtained these points, Bonaparte might have been satisfied, and have approved of a treaty which secured them.[14]

Jefferson himself recognized the bitter truth that British acquiescence in America's demands might well depend upon Napoleon's success. "It is really mortifying," he wrote, "that we should be forced to wish success to Bonaparte and to look to his victories as our salvation." [15]

Herein, of course, lay the tragedy of the situation. Britain's self-interest demanded that she control the high seas, and impressment was, in her judgment, absolutely essential to this control. Equally, the preservation of American honor and sovereignty required the abolition of impressment. Of this the President and the vast majority of his countrymen had no question or doubt. Rufus King, for example, wrote that he "was not sure that Jefferson was not *absolutely obliged*, if he regards the national honor, to send the treaty back." [16] Erskine informed Lord Howicke, the British Foreign Secretary, that:

. . . all parties in this country take a warm Interest on the point of the Non Impressment of sailors (claimed as British) out of American ships on the High Seas, and from every Consideration that I have been able to give the Subject, I am persuaded that no cordiality can be expected from this country whilst it is deemed necessary by His Majesty to enforce the right.[17]

He did suggest that the commercial interests in America favored the treaty, but he said that property had no real influence in a nation where all men could vote. As to the treaty, he continued, the passions of the people had been given prior consideration, and impressment was deemed more important than

---

[14] Pickering to King, January 2, 1808, C. R. King, *The Life and Correspondence of Rufus King* (6 vols., New York, 1898), V, 47.

[15] Jefferson to Taylor, August 1, 1807, A. A. Lipscomb and A. E. Bergh (eds.), *The Writings of Thomas Jefferson* (20 vols., Library Edition, Washington, 1903), XI, 305.

[16] King to Morris, March 30, 1807, King, *The Life and Correspondence of Rufus King*, V, 13.

[17] Erskine to Howick, February 2, 1807, F.O. 5:52.

commercial concessions. This is the kind of situation out of which wars are made, for national interests were diametrically opposed. There was little room for maneuvering when retreat for one meant national destruction, or concession by the other signaled national humiliation. Struggle as both sides might, no escape was found from this deadlock, and its final resolution was sought through war.

Few realized, however, that with the failure of the Monroe-Pinkney treaty the danger of war would increase so swiftly and a crisis would soon arise that would very nearly plunge the United States into the conflict which Jefferson desperately wished to avoid. The Whig ministry of All the Talents was fast approaching its end. Before it went, it took steps to counteract the Berlin Decrees. No government could fail to do otherwise. In January 1807, the cabinet issued an Order in Council which prohibited neutrals from trading between ports owned or occupied by the enemy. This measure was especially injurious to the United States, for it prevented her ships from enjoying the coastal trade where they could choose the markets with the highest prices. There is no question that the measure might have been harsher, for the provocation offered was great. But the order was stringent enough, and the debate that ensued in Parliament gave a rough preview of what could happen if conditions in Europe grew worse. The Tories denounced the measure as catering to American interests and failing to strike a powerful enough blow at the enemy. It would have been better, their spokesmen insisted, if the government had placed an interdict upon all trade from the West Indies to France. They readily admitted that such an interdict might enrage the United States, but an angry America was far less to be feared than a mightier France. And in any event, why should they cater to the interests of the United States? Tory shippers resented the rich profits being reaped by Americans at the expense of honest English merchants. The policies they proposed would add to their own wealth, protect their own economic interests, and restrict the growth of American shipping. All these seemed to be legitimate and desirable goals to many Englishmen.

The government's answer to the attacks upon its program by Perceval and Viscount Castlereagh not only reflected a different view of the world but also revealed the different interests of the groups in society supporting the Whig party. It was not, in the opinion of the Whigs, sensible or practical to outrage the United States. Britain had far too few friends left in the world, and her interests could best be served by retaining the friendship rather than alienating the affections of neutral countries. Further, the manufacturing classes saw in America a substantial market for British goods and were not ready to risk its loss. Through 1807 nearly one third of British exports went to the United States, and only a fool would throw this market to the winds. They admitted that retaliation against Napoleon was necessary; they denied that it should be so severe as to cut off a profitable trade across the Atlantic.

Unfortunately for Jefferson, moderation was overthrown in England, and a new and uncompromising government took over the reins of power. In March 1807, the Whig ministry fell from grace. It had attempted to lift some of the onerous disabilities from Roman Catholics and by doing so encompassed its own downfall. George III would not tolerate such a policy, nor was the country ready for it. The threat from a revolutionary country abroad diminishes the popularity of reform at home. Too often when a society is under attack, it closes ranks and rejects efforts at change as dangerous and subversive. The Whigs were replaced by a vigorous Tory ministry. The Prime Minister was the Duke of Portland, an elderly and undistinguished gentleman. But the cabinet bristled with men of ability and strong views. Perceval, who was to succeed Portland in 1809, was Chancellor of the Exchequer. Castlereagh, who was to become one of Britain's greatest foreign secretaries, was at the War Office. The critical post at the Foreign Office was occupied by Canning. His ability was great, his mind hard and keen, and unfortunately his tongue sharp and wounding. Few men have so earned the hatred of America. That "implacable and rancorous enemy of the United States" wrote John Quincy Adams of him when he died. "May that event," he continued, "avert all the evils which he would, if permitted, have drawn down upon us . . . ." [18] Some of this criticism of Canning was justified,

---

[18] C. F. Adams (ed.), *John Quincy Adams, Memoirs* (12 vols., Philadelphia, 1874–1877), VIII, 328.

for he often seemed to go out of his way to injure. But many of the charges leveled at him were unfair. He did not suffer fools gladly, and he was contemptuous of those less gifted than himself. Yet he served his country loyally and pursued policies that he earnestly believed would best advance her cause. This course of action often brought down abuse upon his head, but he was seldom disturbed. Nor should he have been, for a minister without critics is usually a minister without ability. Behind Canning was Lord Bathurst at the Board of Trade, Lord Hawkesbury (later Lord Liverpool, who became Prime Minister in 1812) at the Home Office, and Lord Mulgrave at the Admiralty. Here was a cabinet that contained three future prime ministers as well as two of the most gifted men to serve in the Foreign Office. They were not easy to deal with, for they had drive, energy, and the determination to fight the war to successful conclusion.

In April 1807, the news of the formation of this new ministry reached America. It followed hard upon the intelligence concerning the Orders in Council and was hardly less welcome. There would be no doubt, as Monroe soon learned from Canning, that few concessions could be wrung from an England under such a government. However, although lines and attitudes were bound to harden, no one expected the sudden eruption over the *Chesapeake* in June of that year. For some time a British squadron had lain at anchor in Chesapeake Bay, waiting to pounce upon several French ships as soon as they had left the sanctuary of American territorial waters. In the course of keeping their station, the British vessels had to send ashore for provisions. Unfortunately, a number of British sailors had used these trips to the mainland to escape from naval service. Even worse, from the British point of view, some of these deserters enlisted in the American navy. Wearing their new uniforms, they nonchalantly strolled down the streets of Norfolk before the exasperated eyes of their old commanding officers. Several of these men were stationed aboard the *Chesapeake*—a fact which its commanding officer, Commodore Barron, was aware of, although he believed that they were American citizens who had been wrongfully impressed into British service. Several attempts were made by Britain to secure the surrender of these deserters, but to no avail. The British consul in Norfolk applied for them, only to be rebuffed by American officials, and Erskine fared no better at the hands of Madison. British tempers were further inflamed when it was learned that French officers were receiving the help of local officials in recapturing sailors who had decided that life in America was preferable to service under Napoleon.

The combination of these circumstances proved too much for Admiral Berkeley, Commander-in-Chief of the British fleet in North American waters. A man with an uncomplicated mind, he chose an uncomplicated solution. On June 1 he issued an order to his officers instructing them, in the event the *Chesapeake* left territorial waters, to stop it, search it, and take from it those of its crew who were British deserters. On June 22 the *Chesapeake* left Hampton Roads and stood out to sea. She was followed at once by *H. M. S. Leopard*, commanded by Captain S. P. Humphrey. Some ten miles off Cape Henry the American frigate was hailed by the British ship and hove to, in order to receive a message delivered by a naval lieutenant. That message consisted of a copy of Admiral Berkeley's instructions and a demand for compliance. The American commodore quite properly refused to allow his ship to be searched and the British officer left the ship. Captain Humphrey then hailed the *Chesapeake* again, saying that his demands must be met. When his orders were ignored, the *Leopard* opened fire on the American frigate and in ten minutes forced her to strike her flag. She was then boarded, and four of her crew were forcibly removed by a search party.

This action was a flagrant violation of American sovereignty. That Captain Humphrey exercised his task with restraint, taking only four sailors when he might have seized more, was quite irrelevant. That the provocation offered British officers was considerable was also irrelevant. The simple facts were that an American public vessel had been stopped, fired upon, members of her crew killed, wounded, and captured. No precedent in international law could justify this action and no stretching of circumstances could make it tolerable. The public outcry against Britain was everything that could have been expected and more. Erskine wrote that "the indignation of the People of

the United States has been excited to the most violent extent
. . . ." Even the "most temperate people and those most at-
tracted to England say that they are bound as a nation and
that they must assert their honour on the first attack upon it,
or subject themselves to an imputation which it may be difficult
to remove." [19] He solemnly added that although it "would be
difficult for any party to induce the Nation to determine upon
a war with England upon Commercial Disputes, or even for the
redress of supposed injuries, yet I am persuaded that the
passions of the people might be worked upon to any extent by
an appeal to them on the Ground of National Insult." [20]

Jefferson, too, saw that opinion was inflamed. This country,
he wrote, "has never been in such a state of excitement since
the battle of Lexington." [21] Indignation was spread as wide as
it was deep. Foster, the British chargé d'affaires, was in New
York at the time and wrote feelingly of the depth of hostility
existing there. Only the Federalists failed to join unanimously in
angry denunciations of Britain. John Lowell of Massachusetts
went so far as to justify the actions of Admiral Berkeley. But
even men of his political persuasion were finally caught up in
the fever sweeping the nation and were compelled, before they
lost all influence, to join in the attacks on Britain.

Had Congress been in session and had Jefferson wished, war
would undoubtedly have come. But the President did not want
to take the final step. There were other ways of securing redress, and these would first be explored. It is true that he told
General Turreau, the French minister, that "if the English do
not give us the satisfaction we demand we will take Canada,
which wants to enter the Union. . . ." Turreau was not convinced of this, however, for he observed that "the President
does not want war and that Mr. Madison dreads it now still
more." Indeed, he went on, if Congress demands war "its
intention will be crossed by powerful intrigue," for the administration "has nothing to gain and everything to lose by

---

[19] Erskine to Canning, No. 18, July 2, 1807, F.O. 5:52.
[20] Erskine to Canning, No. 20, July 17, 1807, F.O. 5:52.
[21] Jefferson to Bowdoin, July 10, 1807, Ford, *The Writings of Thomas Jefferson*, X, 454.

war." [22] Caution then, although some would call it weakness, caused Jefferson to move slowly. Congress was not called back into special session to act in the heat of the moment. Rather, a proclamation was issued on July 2, 1807, expelling all armed British vessels from American waters and prohibiting intercourse with any that refused to leave. The President also concentrated his inadequate gunboats in several East coast ports and warned the states to alert their militia. Further, he discussed the military steps that should be taken if the worst came to worst. Gallatin suggested that the best method of waging a defensive war was to launch an attack upon Canada. The War Hawks were not the first to see the advantages of invading Britain's North American provinces.

But time was first given to Britain to make amends. Jefferson wrote:

The fact is what they have to settle with us. Reason & the usage of civilized nations require that we should give them an opportunity of disavowal & reparation. Our own interests too, the very means of making war, requires that we should give time to our merchants to gather in their vessels & property & our seamen now afloat.[23]

Therefore instructions were sent to England via the *Revenge* calling upon the British government for "reparations for the past outrage and security for the future . . . ." [24] More specifically, Monroe was instructed to insist upon a "formal disavowal of the deed, and restoration of the four seamen to the ship from which they were taken . . . ." Linked to this and as a "security for the future" was the additional demand for "an entire abolition of impressments from vessels under the flag of the United States . . . ." [25]

It was the joining of these issues that made subsequent negotiations so difficult and so protracted. A settlement of the

---

[22] Turreau to Tallyrand, July 18, 1807, quoted Henry Adams, *History of the United States during the Administrations of Jefferson and Madison* (9 vols., New York, 1889–1891), IV, 36.

[23] Jefferson to Epps, July 12, 1807, Ford, *The Writings of Thomas Jefferson*, X, 457–458.

[24] Jefferson to Namours, *ibid.*, X, 460.

[25] Madison to Monroe, July 6, 1807, Gaillard Hunt, *The Writings of James Madison* (7 vols., New York, 1900–1910), VII, 455–456.

Chesapeake affair was, of itself, not insuperable. Indeed, Canning had, at the first informal news of the attack, informed Monroe that Britain had never "maintained the pretensions of a right to search ships of war . . . for deserters." [26] He also said that if the British officers "should prove to have been culpable, the most prompt and effectual reparation shall be afforded to the Government of the United States." [27] Thus an immediate apology and swift reparations could have been arranged. That this did not take place was due entirely to the insertion into the talks of the impressment issue. Monroe saw Canning four days after receiving his instructions and presented America's demands. He was not cheered by the reception he was given. The British Foreign Secretary suggested that the United States had already taken a measure of redress by excluding British ships of war from American waters. And he categorically refused to link impressment with the settlement of the whole affair. He was, he said, quite prepared to enter into separate conversations on impressment, but he would never take part in any discussion that joined the one with the other. There the interview ended.

On September 23 Canning sent a lengthy note to Monroe outlining the British government's attitude toward the American claims for reparations. He repeated the charge that the Proclamation of July 2 was in itself an act of redress and must affect the British offer of reparation. He inquired whether the United States intended to withdraw the Proclamation now that his government had disavowed the actions of Admiral Berkeley. He suggested that although there could be no justification for the actions of the *Leopard*, there were extenuating circumstances that might place the entire affair in a slightly different light. Finally, he insisted that impressment be treated as an issue separate and distinct from the *Chesapeake* affair. If, Canning observed, Monroe's instructions bound him to connect the two, there could be no sense in continuing discussions in England. Instead, the British minister said, the entire matter would

---

[26] Canning to Monroe, August 3, 1807, *American State Papers, Foreign Relations*, III, 188.

[27] Canning to Monroe, July 25, 1807, *ibid.*, III, 187.

be placed in the hand of a special envoy to the United States—
an envoy expressly forbidden to deal with the matter of impressment from merchant vessels. As Monroe's instructions did
in fact require a settlement of impressment as part of the general
agreement, George Henry Rose was appointed as the special
representative to Washington.

Before Rose arrived in America, the last futile discussions
were held on the now moribund Monroe-Pinkney Treaty. Although rejected by Jefferson because it had failed to include
an article on impressment, an effort had been made in the
summer of 1807 to renew discussions on the subject. In July
Monroe and Pinkney had expressed the hope to Canning that
new efforts might secure "a more satisfactory result" than what
had been achieved in December 1806. [28] Talks over the *Chesapeake* affair postponed these discussions until October when
the two Americans met Canning. Two days before this last
meeting the British government issued a proclamation calling
upon all British seamen to quit foreign service and ship aboard
British vessels and authorizing the impressment of all seamen
who failed to comply with this order. The news of this step
horrified Monroe and Pinkney, and they were quick to say to
Canning that they hoped that this proclamation was not designed
to "shut the door against negotiations and concession . . . ."
Canning said it was not intended to have this effect, but rather
that it was simply a statement of principles and practices that
the British government held to be warranted by "public law
& long established usage." However, he added, there was no
prospect that Britain would give up impressment on the high
seas. He emphasized that the "present state of the world, and
the nature and mode of that hostility which France is now waging against this country . . . rendered it to the last degree
hazardous, if not absolutely impracticable, to stipulate for the
abandonment of a practice to which the navy and the people
of England attach so much importance." [29] Three days later
Canning abruptly ended all talks by saying that in any event
the proposal to renew negotiations on a treaty "already solemnly

---

[28] Monroe and Pinkney to Canning, July 24, 1807, *ibid.*, III, 194.
[29] Monroe and Pinkney to Madison, October 22, 1807, *ibid.*, III, 196.

concluded and signed is . . . wholly inadmissible." [30]

Monroe had nothing left to do but sail for home. His hopes, his aspirations, and his treaty lay in ruins about him. The *Chesapeake* affair was left unresolved to work its harm upon the two countries. But Monroe and Pinkney had done all that mind and energy could do. They had talked and bargained endlessly. They had made concessions when compromise was necessary, and they had stood firm when a retreat from principles would have betrayed their country. And they had failed. Yet that failure was not the result of lack of skill or determination. Rather it came about because Britain's wartime position made it impossible for her to offer meaningful concessions to the United States. Impressment was the rock on which the negotiations foundered, just as it was the bulwark upon which the Royal Navy built its strength. This conflict of interest was to drive America and Britain farther and farther apart.

Jefferson had delayed taking serious retaliatory action while he awaited news from London about the *Chesapeake*. The Proclamation of July 2 was only a mild and moderate measure, despite Canning's efforts to stigmatize it as being otherwise. But the President could not wait much longer. In June the country had been united behind him and ready for strong and decisive action. Now the end of the year was fast approaching and not a hint of reparation had been made. Congress was to meet in October, and a policy of inaction would be difficult to maintain and impossible to justify. The only questions now concerned the nature and severity of the measures to be taken against Britain. And here the months of delay worked to weaken the President's hand. Actions taken when emotions were running high could have been swift and direct. But anger is difficult to sustain unless the injury is flagrant and continuing. The passage of time had cooled the ardor of many and had allowed opponents of Jefferson to reorganize their forces. Although the President might now have felt that war was desirable, too many elements in the country did not share such a sentiment. A retaliation short of war was the only solution. The President did admit that despite any action he might take war could

---

[30] Canning to Monroe and Pinkney, October 22, 1807, *ibid.*, III, 199.

still come. In September he observed that a "war with England was probable," [31] and a few days later he wrote that it could be inferred from Berkeley's orders that a "war with us had been predetermined." [32] Nevertheless, it would not be he who forced the issue. Restrictions on trade, a favored and familiar method, would first be tried.

On December 14 the long-delayed nonimportation act went into effect. Passed in 1806 and suspended while the Monroe-Pinkney negotiations dragged on, the time had come for it to be enforced. But the rush of events in Europe had already rendered it out of date. It was not just that the *Chesapeake* affair was unresolved, or that Britain's proclamation on impressment had been issued. Far more crucial were the news of the Berlin Decrees and the intimations of Britain's reaction to them. Napoleon's defeat of Russia had allowed France to incorporate most of Europe into her continental system. The threat now posed to Britain was so grave that she turned to her famous Orders in Council for salvation. In reply to Napoleon's blockade of the British Isles, London closed off all trade to areas that excluded the British flag. Britain did permit neutrals to trade from enemy ports to certain designated British ports, and she did permit license trade with Europe, but that was the extent of her concessions. To counteract these measures, France issued the Milan Decrees which called for the seizure of any neutral vessel abiding by the Orders in Council. It was in the light of these hazardous circumstances, not all of which were definitely known until 1808 but most of which were expected earlier, that the President had to act. The problem he faced was how to devise effective means to cope with both these real and anticipated dangers. If the nonimportation act were insufficient—and it was—perhaps a more sweeping and radical economic step might answer. And what better than an embargo? It would secure American vessels from depredations abroad; it would punish Britain by denying her supplies; and it would uphold American honor by retaliating against those who would injure

---

[31] Jefferson to Madison, September 21, 1807, Ford, *The Writings of Thomas Jefferson*, X, 489.

[32] Jefferson to Paine, September 6, 1807, Ford, *ibid.*, X, 493.

America. Further, all this would be done without the serious risk of war, which is why an embargo had such appeal to a cautious Secretary of State, a puzzled and even divided Congress, and a pacific President.

Once the decision had been taken to recommend an embargo, events moved rapidly. The cabinet met to discuss the measure on December 17. Although Gallatin expressed some reservations about Jefferson's proposal, a modified bill was quickly agreed upon. On the following day the President sent a message to Congress. In it he spoke of the hazards to which American seamen and ships were exposed and proposed that an "inhibition of the departure of our vessels from the ports of the United States" be implemented. If the executive acted swiftly, the legislature was not far behind. The Senate, with only six dissenting votes, passed the act in one afternoon. John Quincy Adams, although reluctant to support the bill, realized that vigorous action was necessary and that private interest must, in his words, "not be put in opposition to public good." [33] The House of Representatives did not show quite the same dispatch. Here more reservations were expressed about the wisdom of the bill, and more opposition was voiced to its enactment. But the weight of support for the President together with the need for decision overwhelmed the detractors of the bill. By a vote of 82 to 44 it was enacted into law. Only four days after the original message was sent to Congress the President signed the bill.

Both in its conception and in its execution the embargo was a two-edged sword. It was designed to protect American interests and to coerce the European belligerents into making the concessions that Americans felt were their due. In his message to Congress, Jefferson said that American ships and their seamen were being threatened on the high seas and that he was recommending an embargo to "keep in safety these essential resources . . . ." [34] Madison instructed Pinkney to in-

---

[33] W. C. Ford (ed.), *The Writings of John Quincy Adams* (7 vols., New York, 1914), III, 168–169, n. 2.

[34] J. D. Richardson, *A Compilation of the Messages and Papers of the Presidents 1789–1897* (20 vols., Washington, 1900).

form Canning that the embargo was a "measure of precaution only" and that it should not be considered "hostile in its character . . . ." [35] The Secretary of State also told Erskine specifically that "this act was not intended as a Measure of Hostility against Great Britain, but only as a precaution against the risk their shipping would run in the present extraordinary State of their Relations with the belligerent Nations . . . ." [36] But despite these protestations about the self-denying nature of the act, it was quite clear that one of its major purposes was to force Britain to alter her policies. Pickering wrote that "the Embargo is unquestionably levelled at Britain," and he was right.[37] For the first to suffer would be Britain and her colonies. This was made particularly clear in March 1808 when a supplemental act aimed directly at Canada was passed. If the embargo had been designed only to protect American ships on the high seas, why prohibit trade by land with Canada? Yet the new measure prohibited "in any manner whatever" the export of goods banned in the Act of December 22, 1807. If such commodities were in fact sent out of the country either "by land or water," heavy penalties were to be imposed upon the guilty party.[38] Exceptions were to be made for the fur trade because the administration heeded Erskine's pleas that commerce be permitted with the Indians. In any event, this trade had been guaranteed by Jay's Treaty, and it would have been difficult to abolish it.

Despite this permissive action, incidents flared up along the border. Bateaux of the Michilimachinac Company containing supplies were seized at the mouth of the Niagara River, causing a real and anticipated loss of thousands of pounds. In Passamaquoddy Bay American troops occupied Moose Island and seized a vessel that was carrying flour after it had called at Deer Island. Further incidents took place at Oswego and Sackett's Harbor. Indeed, the lawlessness of the frontier became so

---

[35] Madison to Pinkney, December 23, 1807, *American State Papers, Foreign Relations*, III, 206.

[36] Erskine to Canning, No. 31, December 23, 1807, F.O. 5:52.

[37] Pickering to King, January 2, 1808, King, *The Life and Correspondence of Rufus King*, V, 45.

[38] *Annals of Congress*, 10th Congress, 1st Session, 2839–2842.

blatant and the enforcement of the embargo so difficult that the President issued a proclamation calling upon all citizens to aid in the suppression of "insurrections and combinations which flouted the law." [39] The disturbances in the northern portion of the country were symptomatic of the distress felt in the nation as a whole. A measure like the embargo had to have the wholehearted support of the people if it were to be effective. If it were received like prohibition—whose purpose was opposed and whose enforcement was flouted—it would fail ignominiously. Unfortunately for Jefferson, just as the great twentieth-century experiment to make and keep all Americans sober collapsed in indignity, so the embargo which was designed to teach the world that Americans could rise above material considerations to protect their honor also crashed in ruins. In doing so it showed the paucity of the President's policy and left his successor the unenviable task of finding new alternatives that would impress Britain and France with the need to moderate their policies.

The failure of the embargo and the destruction of a great experiment in morality began almost as soon as the law was passed. In the early portion of 1808 the House of Representatives attached to a bill a rider that permitted American owners with property abroad to send, after submitting proof to the government, ships to secure them. This was broadly interpreted as allowing American merchants who had contracted for foreign goods before the act to send American goods in payment for these commodities. The President acquiesced in this practice and had from the very beginning issued to individuals permits that allowed them to do so. But an act to alleviate honest distress soon became a device to avoid commercial loss. Nearly six hundred American vessels sailed overseas in the first months of the embargo; at least four hundred of them had returned by the end of the year with foreign cargoes. American exports were, therefore, continuing to find a place in Britain, and English goods were still filling American markets. But overseas trade was just one of the breaches in the act. Ships strayed into the West Indies in order to repair fictitious damage to

---

[39] Richardson, *Messages and Papers of the Presidents,* I, 450–451.

their equipment. Coastal traders found themselves well served by violent storms that took place in unaccountably calm weather and drove their ships into Canadian ports. Indeed, so enormously did illicit trade with British North America develop, that in 1808 exports from the St. Lawrence were double the average of the preceding five years. This trade reached such a flood that Canadian merchants began to complain of being inundated with American goods. The deputy collector of the port of Boston wrote Jefferson saying that "it is painfull to me to relate that notwithstanding the care of the Custom House to prevent all abuses against the embargo laws we have failed of the wishes for success." [40] To stop these violations, Gallatin proposed punishing measures that would have empowered the executive arm of the government to enforce its will; but Jefferson did not take this step until January 1809. Then legislation was passed enabling the government to make anticipatory seizures, to refuse the loading of vessels without government permission, and to place the onus of proof for straying into foreign ports upon the offending owner. This extraordinary legislation was received with a proper measure of outrage. The country had suffered enough already.

New England had borne the brunt of the effects of the embargo. One journalist wrote of Boston: "What is the huge forest of dry trees that spreads itself before the town? You behold the masts of ships thrown out of employment by the embargo." [41] Exports, the very lifeblood of Northeastern shippers, dropped catastrophically. In the period from October 1807 to October 1808, exports were some eighty-six million dollars less than in the preceding years. Not until after the War of 1812 would exports again reach the total that was set from 1806 to 1807. Indeed, in the best intervening year, 1810, they were only slightly over half what they had been in 1806. The problems of New England were also the problems of the other states to the south and west. Cotton prices were cut in half, and

---

[40] *Letters from the Collector*, Boston, July 19, 1808, I, 203, quoted L. D. White, *The Jeffersonians—A Study in Administrative History 1801–1829* (New York, 1951), 444.

[41] *New York Evening Post*, February 24, 1809, quoted A. T. Mahan, *Sea Power in its Relation to the War of 1812* (London, 1905), I, 194.

planters were hard pressed. Prices for the crops of Western farmers did not fall as sharply as did prices of cotton, but they fell low enough to cause serious discomfort for the well-to-do farmers and disaster for the marginal farmers. Ports like New Orleans and Savannah were crowded with ships lying idle at the docks. The surprising thing, as Erskine wrote, was the support given to the embargo by areas such as New York, Philadelphia, and Baltimore.

Distress at home might have been endured if the embargo had worked its magic abroad. But this was demonstrably untrue. A combination of good fortune and shrewd foresight had kept British exports at a most satisfactory level. Some goods still went to the United States, but even more were shipped to the Spanish-American market, which was just opening up. Although British exports to the United States in 1808 were roughly half what they had been in 1807, the value of goods sent to South America in the year of the embargo was more than 50 per cent above that of the preceding year. What was lost on the swings was being gained on the roundabouts. It is true that pressure in England was building up against the Orders in Council and some sympathy for the United States did exist. But the commercial classes who felt that concessions should be made to America were lacking in power and influence. Tory landowners and shippers rather than Whig merchants controlled Parliament and the government, and as long as they did, they would rejoice in America's distress and remain convinced that she could be treated with contempt.

Although England remained obdurate, forces opposed to the embargo in America were gathering strength and giving voice to their objections. In April 1808, Congress passed legislation empowering the President to lift the embargo from whichever belligerent first removed its commercial restrictions or from both if they acted simultaneously. The passage of this act involved the United States in a long and unsuccessful attempt to persuade England to rescind the Orders in Council. Similarly fruitless efforts were directed at France in the hope of gaining the repeal of the Berlin and Milan Decrees. The proposals made by the United States were fully exploited by the European belligerents, neither of whom had any intention of accepting the American offer, but both of whom were prepared to use it to further their own ends. Napoleon coldly rejected the offer, and Champagny, the French Foreign Minister, wrote John Armstrong, the American minister in Paris, that the United States should be eager to avenge the insults offered her by the Orders in Council. In fact, he said, Napoleon really considered that a state of war existed between America and Britain. This was the extent of the sympathy that Washington received from France.

England proved equally immune to the blandishments from the United States. Pinkney, the American minister in London, informed the British Foreign Secretary that if Britain lifted her Orders in Council and thus "entitled" herself to the suspension of the embargo, the United States would offer "just resistance" to France's "irregularities." At the same time, he said that the renewed intercourse between Britain and America "would open the way for a return to good understanding" between their two countries.[42] Though the suggestion was rejected, Pinkney continued to press his case. Finally in September he received a crushing reply to his advances. His Majesty's government could not consent, Canning wrote, "to buy off that hostility which ought not to have been extended to him, at the expense of a concession made, not to America, but to France." He further observed, with the bland self-righteousness which was so infuriating, that if the embargo "is only to be considered as an innocent municipal regulation which affects none but the United States themselves," there could be "not only no reciprocity, but no assignable relation between the repeal, by the United States of a measure of voluntary self-restriction and the surrender by His Majesty, of his right of retaliation against his enemies."[43]

Britain's determination to stand fast was reinforced by Erskine's reports that internal opposition to the embargo was so powerful that the measure might soon be withdrawn. And he was right. In November, when Congress met, opposition to

---

[42] Pinkney to Madison, August 4, 1808, *American State Papers, Foreign Relations,* III, 249.
[43] Canning to Pinkney, September 23, 1808, *ibid.,* III, 231.

CHAPTER III

The Search for Alternatives

THE FAILURE OF THE EMBARGO and the introduction of a new nonintercourse act opened up a bleak vista for the United States. America had been frustrated in her efforts to end impressment and she had failed in her attempts to have the Orders in Council withdrawn. Neither negotiations nor coercion had affected the European belligerents, and America was hard pressed to know where to turn. However, since war was still unthinkable, continued talks rather than resort to force were still to be preferred. What real hope there was lay in the new administration of President Madison. He had the advantage of familiarity with the problems at hand, for he had served as Jefferson's Secretary of State. But knowledge alone of the difficulties would not bring about their solution. This would require skill, determination, and a firm grasp of the possible. These qualities Madison did not display in abundance. He was often uncertain and frequently could be swayed by conflicting advice. His choice in appointments lacked discernment and he sometimes preferred weak men rather than run the risk of battling strong personalities. For example, he named Robert Smith as Secretary of State when that office needed a man of stature rather than a mediocrity who could hardly draft his own dispatches. But if Madison lacked the ability to fire the enthusiasm of his countrymen and if he lacked the resources to provide imaginative leadership, it was also true that circumstances were against him. Again and again it was the weakness of the United States that shaped policies in Washington. Under the best of circumstances it is not easy to play the cards of a neutral nation caught in the crush between two great powers.

It is almost impossible to do it successfully when that neutral country's power is minimal and the support of its population uncertain.

The pressures under which Madison found himself when he assumed office were very great. Impressment continued to rob America of her seamen, and the pace of commercial warfare continued unabated. The inflexibility of Britain concerning impressment forced the United States to concentrate on securing relief from commercial warfare. But before relief could be secured, there remained important business to finish. Chief of these was the *Chesapeake* affair. In 1807 when Jefferson was still President, the British had sent George Henry Rose to settle this damaging problem. Canning had insisted that no reparation could be made until the United States agreed to separate the issue of impressment from the negotiations. This the Americans agreed to do. Canning also insisted that Jefferson's proclamation to be withdrawn before discussions were undertaken. But this was an impossible demand and Rose was prepared to seek a compromise on it. But the British envoy's additional demands, which included a suggestion that the Americans make an effort to return to Britain all British-born deserters, proved too much for the Secretary of State. He rejected it out of hand and now Rose felt that he had no choice but to terminate his mission. He did so in March 1808.

Although Rose had failed, Erskine continued to work hard for an improvement in Anglo-American relations. He had reported to London that the continued enforcement of the Orders in Council could lead to war. This opinion did not carry much weight in London, however. What did influence Canning was Erskine's report on the nonintercourse act, which was to replace the embargo. This act, it was pointed out, would place Britain and France on the same footing so that the cry of discrimination against England could no longer be justified. Further, Erskine had held several long and revealing discussions with Gallatin toward the end of the year 1808. In them, he said, the Secretary of the Treasury had suggested that the United States would put an end to the practice of receiving British deserters aboard American ships of war and that Congress was considering legislation to enforce the termination of this practice by merchant ships. He also said that Gallatin intimated that the United States might accept the Rule of 1756—something that Gallatin later denied. Finally, Erskine quoted Gallatin as saying, "You see, Sir, we could settle a treaty in my Private Room in two Hours which might perhaps be found to be as lasting as if it had been bound up in all the formality of a regular system . . . ."[1]

Canning received this news in London with every evidence of pleasure and soon met with Pinkney to discuss developments. The new nonintercourse act, he suggested, removed the impediment to a settlement of the *Chesapeake* affair. He said that in the light of new circumstances it might be possible to bring the *Chesapeake* matter to a satisfactory conclusion, along with the embargo and the Orders in Council. He even discussed with Pinkney the terms that he would lay down. Pinkney recommended that he send these to Erskine and so the negotiations were begun. What then followed was little short of disastrous, for a settlement approached with high optimism and concluded with warm good will was rudely rejected by Canning. And what could have been a major step in the *rapprochement* between the two powers turned into a bitter wrangle that drove them farther apart.

Canning first directed Erskine to deal with the *Chesapeake* problem. Then he laid down three conditions for the repeal of the Orders in Council. They were that the United States withdraw all restrictions now applied to British ships and trade, that she recognize the Rule of 1756, and that she permit British naval forces to capture American vessels trading with France in violation of the law of the United States. If the first two conditions were difficult, the last was downright offensive, for it gave Britain the right to enforce Congressional legislation—a right which was odious to the United States and presumptuous on the part of England.

Notwithstanding these problems, rapid progress was made. After a certain amount of bargaining, an agreement on the *Chesapeake* case was reached. Smith, the Secretary of State, wanted further punishment of Admiral Berkeley, but the British

---

[1] Erskine to Canning, No. 47, December 4, 1808, F.O. 5:58.

minister said a reprimand was serious enough and that his government felt that it was going as far as it could in returning the survivors of that action as well as paying compensation to the families of the victims. Rather than protract this already exhausting debate, Smith agreed to these terms and this vexatious issue seemed finally resolved. The repeal of the Orders in Council was more difficult and Erskine had given much thought to Canning's conditions. He anticipated no difficulty over the first one, for the new nonintercourse act would cover it. However, he believed that recognition of the Rule of 1756 and the use of British ships to enforce American law were bound to be tricky. This conviction proved to be well founded, for Smith argued that although the United States might acquiesce in the Rule of 1756, formal recognition of it could only be embodied in a general commercial treaty. As for the last condition, the Secretary of State insisted that a stipulation that Britain could enforce American law would be degrading to the United States and would be attended with no advantage to Britain.

Erskine was placed in a most difficult position. He was loath to depart from his instructions, but he was equally reluctant to let a settlement slip through his fingers. He decided, therefore, to ignore the letter of his instructions and follow their spirit. There were, he said, "considerations of great weight" that urged him to make an adjustment of the "differences between the two countries." [2] A new Congress was soon to meet; if an agreement were not reached before its sitting, Erskine feared that radically new steps might be taken against Britain. He was also convinced that America and France were drawing farther apart and that he could accelerate this development by reaching a quick accord with the United States. Because of these factors, he concluded a settlement with Smith.

On April 18, 1809, Erskine wrote the Secretary of State that an envoy extraordinary would be sent to conclude a treaty and that in the meantime the British government would withdraw the Orders in Council as they respected the United States in the "persuasion that the President would issue a proclamation

---

[2] Erskine to Canning, No. 20, April 20, 1809, F.O. 5:63.

for the renewal of the intercourse with Britain." [3] Receiving a warm reply from Smith that the President would do this, Erskine then replied that the Orders in Council would be lifted on June 10. He was informed, in turn, that trade with Britain would also be reopened that day. The publication of this settlement cheered Americans who felt that Britain was finally beginning to modify the practices that had so burdened the United States. Some thought that the concessions were the result of the embargo, but whether this view was correct or not, there was, in the words of Erskine, "universal satisfaction" at the turn in events.[4] Vessels that had long lain idle set sail for England. Such was their number that between June 16 and 23 more cotton was landed at Liverpool than in most of 1807. In addition to the ships that sailed in the confident knowledge that all was well, another six hundred vessels were being prepared for overseas voyages. Enthusiasm for the new economic prosperity ran high. The news of further allied setbacks in Spain convinced even more Americans that Britain's government would consider the interests of the United States with increased respect and deference. As a result of this friendly atmosphere, Smith began to talk of a settlement of impressment. He observed that the United States could make regulations that would prevent British seamen from being employed aboard American vessels and would provide for the surrender of British deserters already on American ships. These regulations would make impressment unnecessary. He added that he did not expect Britain to "abandon the Principle, but only the Practice of Impressment out of American Ships." [5] Nothing could have been more amiable.

But, of course, it was a fool's paradise, for Erskine's agreement was to be repudiated in London. An intimation that all was not well first came with the news of the modified Orders in Council of April 1809. Pressure was building up in England

---

[3] Erskine to Smith, *American State Papers, Class 1, Foreign Relations,* III, 296.

[4] Erskine to Canning, No. 22, May 4, 1809, F.O. 5:63.

[5] Erskine to Canning, No. 29, July 3, 1809, F.O. 5:63.

to alter the original decrees to meet new circumstances. Spain, Portugal, and Turkey were now allies of Britain, and trade to them should no longer have to go through the United Kingdom. Further, it was the opinion of Alexander Baring, an influential merchant with strong American connections, and of a large number of Whigs that concessions might now usefully be made to the United States. The news of the lifting of the embargo provided the government with the opportunity to announce changes, for now it could make changes without risking the charge that British policy was being tailored to fit American complaints. Certainly Canning viewed the news from America as justifying British firmness, and the changes that he supported, while granting certain concessions, were designed to meet British needs far more than American interests. The new policy provided for a strict blockade of Europe from the Ems to Italy. Trade with French colonies was absolutely forbidden, but Germany and the Baltic were to be opened to neutral commerce. In addition, the cost of licenses to trade in Europe was reduced and the duties on goods in transit through Britain were lowered or abolished.

The new orders pleased Pinkney who thought that his country's interests were being better served. This opinion was shared by some hostile critics of the British government who thought that too much had been given the United States. But although some measure of conciliation had been made, it was far less significant than Pinkney supposed. The interdiction of trade with French colonies was a hard blow, and the limited opening of trade to Europe was far less liberal than might be thought. The truth is that the substance of British policy remained unchanged.

The continuation of a rigid commercial policy rather than Erskine's optimistic liberalism accurately reflected British intentions. This revelation came with enormous clarity when Erskine's agreement reached London, for Canning repudiated it and recalled the British minister. This single act, as unexpected as it was unwelcome, took America by surprise, and it struck a terrible blow at the understanding that appeared to be developing between the two countries. The consequences of this step by the Foreign Secretary can hardly be overestimated. At one stroke Canning threw away a settlement of the *Chesapeake* affair; made impossible the withdrawal of the nonintercourse act by America and the Orders in Council by England; and repelled a hopeful move to reach agreement on impressment. These costs were high enough. But more was to be paid, for the repudiation of Erskine left a bitter distrust of British diplomacy in American minds and cast a long shadow over all future negotiations. Jefferson despaired of any future accommodation with the British; he believed that they "intended seriously to claim the ocean as their conquest, and think to amuse us with embassies and negotiations, until the claim shall be strengthened by time and exercise, and the moment arrive when they may boldly avow what hitherto they have only squinted at." [6] Madison, too, concluded that Britain no longer wished "to put an end to differences from which such advantages are extracted . . . ." [7]

Why did Canning act as he did? His own explanation was simple. Erskine, he insisted, had exceeded his instructions and signed an agreement that did not conform to the government's policies or interests. In a long dispatch the Foreign Secretary elaborated on these charges. As to the *Chesapeake* agreement, he said, a basic stipulation for settlement had been the exclusion of French ships of war from American ports. Of this, Canning wrote, "you appear to have taken no notice whatever . . . ." Further, he charged that Erskine had not secured a repeal of the Proclamation of 1807, although Canning was aware that the nonintercourse act repealed the law upon which the proclamation rested. Finally, he criticized the British minister for accepting a note from Smith "so full of disrespect to His Majesty . . . ." [8] He was equally sharp on the agreement to suspend the Orders in Council. The three conditions which had been laid down for a settlement, he wrote, have not been met. The withdrawal of the nonintercourse and nonimportation

---

[6] Jefferson to Madison, September 12, 1809, A. A. Lipscomb and A. E. Bergh (eds.), *The Writings of Thomas Jefferson* (20 vols., Library Edition, Washington, 1903), XII, 311.

[7] Madison to Jay, January 17, 1810, Gaillard Hunt (ed.), *The Writings of James Madison* (7 vols., New York, 1900–1910), VIII, 88.

[8] Canning to Erskine, No. 10, May 22, 1809, F.O. 5:63.

acts applied to Britain and the enforcement against France
should have been consigned to a formal and written agreement,
for otherwise America could have rescinded these measures
without infringing the agreement. Quite as serious was Erskine's
failure to secure American recognition of the Rule of 1756 and
American acquiescence in the use of the Royal Navy to enforce
its own laws on the high seas.

Unhappily, all these accusations had substance to them. Even
Madison admitted that "Erskine is in a ticklish situation with
Govt. I suspect he will not be able to defend himself against
the charge of exceeding his instructions . . . ."[9] Lord Bathurst
of the Board of Trade was of the opinion that Erskine had exceeded his powers and that Britain was not, therefore, bound to
ratify the treaty. If the agreement had really served Britain's
interests, the government would have tolerated Erskine's departure from his written instructions. But, in the opinion of
the cabinet, it did not, so the disavowal was doubly necessary.
Britain was not prepared to breach her economic blockade
of Europe. Marginal concessions might be made to America (as
they were in the new Orders in Council), but not major ones.
And if it were only major concessions that the United States
would accept, then she would get nothing. An angry and
bellicose America was a more tolerable proposition to Canning
than a weakened Britain. His judgment could well have been
wrong, of course, for it might have been better to have con-
ciliated the United States and to have made her a friendly
neutral. But most Englishmen did not believe this in 1809. And
one cannot be certain that they were wrong. Undoubtedly the
debacle of Erskine's making sharpened the differences between
Britain and America. But the repeal of the Orders in Council
would not have ended Anglo-American disputes. It might only
have whetted Washington's appetite for a settlement of impressment. And Britain's proclamation on that subject in 1807, as
Adams said, "has given a new and darker complexion to our
old controversies."[10]

---

[9] Madison to Jefferson, August 16, 1809, Hunt, *The Writings of James Madison*, VIII, 67.

[10] J. Q. Adams to J. Adams, December 27, 1807, W. C. Ford, *The Writings of John Quincy Adams* (7 vols., New York, 1914), III, 169.

If Canning had some justification for disavowing Erskine, he had none for his subsequent behavior. It was his duty to replace the recalled minister with a man of tact and wisdom who would be able to salvage something from the wreckage. Instead of doing so he appointed Francis James Jackson, a man who possessed to a fatal degree all the qualities that irritated Americans. In 1802 Rufus King had called Jackson "positive, vain, and intolerant." [11] When he heard of his appointment in 1809 he wrote that the new minister's "temper was not mild, nor were his manners conciliatory, his Integrity and Talents were unquestioned, but no proof had yet been disclosed of his prudence." [12] Jackson's discretion was soon to be tested, and he showed that he had not changed from the day when he had moved George III to wonder why, at the bombardment of Copenhagen, the Prince Royal of Denmark had not kicked him down the stairs. Jackson landed at Annapolis in September 1809 and proceeded to Washington where he awaited the President's return from his summer home. During this period he observed the American scene and wrote home spacious descriptions of the horrors that greeted his eyes. He noted that irritation over commercial issues existed in America but added that "they have been strongly worked upon by every Sort of Artifice, of Misrepresentation, and of Falsehood, which the American Democrat or the French Partisan could devise for the purpose." [13] It is little wonder that when he finally met with officials in Washington to discuss a settlement, the gulf was widened between Britain and America.

Jackson's instructions were explicit and rigid. He was to propose reparations for the attack on the *Chesapeake* but to offer to lift the Orders in Council only if Erskine's three original conditions were met. In addition, Canning put the blame on America for Erskine's failure by suggesting that Washington had induced him to depart from his instructions. This was cold comfort to a country seething with indignation. If the Foreign Secretary's comments had been softened by grace or wit,

---

[11] King to the Secretary of State, No. 62, April 10, 1802, C. R. King, *The Life and Correspondence of Rufus King* (6 vols., New York, 1898), IV, 150.
[12] King to Pickering, December 25, 1809, *ibid.*, V, 177.
[13] Jackson to Canning, No. 2, September 13, 1809, F.O. 5:64.

they would have been difficult to take. Presented as they were with an elephantine force, they were insufferable. Consequently, the exchanges between Smith and Jackson became more and more heated, until Jackson finally charged that Erskine had violated his instructions with the full knowledge of the American government. This was too much to bear, and Smith curtly replied that he would accept no further communications from the British minister. Congress heartily approved this step and passed a resolution stating that Jackson's charges were "highly indecorous and insolent—their repetition still more insolent and affronting . . . ." [14]

Instead of returning home promptly, Jackson compounded his folly by touring the country visiting men of "Wealth and Respectability." They were, he felt compelled to admit, "very warm" in their attachment to Britain.[15] He did run into hostility in New York but attributed that to unruly Irishmen. He was invited to New England but in a fit of good sense refrained from going, for his visit might have influenced the coming election. Until he sailed for England, he remained in New York and sunned himself in a Federalist climate, certain that he had acted correctly, convinced that men of intelligence supported England, and fearful only that men of good sense would not be able to restrain the vulgar politicians in Washington from going to war.

With the departure of Jackson from Washington, a new stage was reached in Anglo-American relations. The conduct of American foreign policy had never been easy; it now became more difficult than ever. The war in Europe was going badly for Britain, and internal disputes within the old government had brought about the formation of a new cabinet which was resolute in its determination to reverse the tide of defeat in Europe. The events that triggered the creation of a new ministry sprang from the growing hostility between Canning and Castlereagh. Castlereagh finally resigned from the government, challenged Canning to a duel, and wounded him in the encounter that followed. In the subsequent governmental shuffle, the old

---

[14] *Annals of Congress,* 11th Congress, 1st and 2nd Sessions, I, 481.

[15] Jackson to Bathurst, No. 2, January 22, 1810, F.O. 5:69.

Prime Minister was replaced by Perceval, the chief author of the Orders in Council. The Foreign Office was given to Lord Wellesley whose experience in India and whose natural sloth made him an unlikely vehicle for the appeasement of America. Lord Liverpool, a staunch supporter of British maritime rights, became Secretary of State for War and the Colonies. All in all it was not a cabinet from which the United States could draw comfort.

External circumstances were not much more auspicious. Erskine had been repudiated in Britain, and Jackson had been rejected in Washington. The embargo had been withdrawn, but the nonintercourse act could hardly be expected to succeed where stronger measures had failed. The *Chesapeake* affair still acted as an abrasive on the relations between the two countries. The complexity of the problems that faced America and the seeming impossibility of devising weapons to coerce the European powers created a lack of direction—at times a virtual paralysis—in both the Presidency and Congress. The hard fact was that the protection of the country's interests would be expensive. The United States would have to increase the size of its army, expand its navy, and raise taxes. But while the President could ask for the increase in armed forces, Congress was not prepared to push for the new taxes. Its members would argue the merits of the case and insist that strong steps should be taken, but in the final analysis a majority of them lacked the fundamental desire to cut out of the tangled thicket they were caught in. And it was not just for lack of courage. Some Congressmen were, of course, men of narrow vision, but most were simply overwhelmed by the enormity of their problems. It is cheap and easy to talk about waging war and winning victory; it is rather more difficult to pursue policies that might plunge your country—unprepared and divided—into armed conflict. For this reason confusion reigned in the halls of Congress and men still sought a peaceful solution to their problems. By 1810, however, there was a rising group of intellectually vigorous politicians who had tired of negotiation and discussion, who were becoming convinced that honor and pride should be placed at the forefront, and who were certain that only force would resolve America's problems. But before they could alter their country's course, two or more years of intricate maneuvering were to take place.

In the meantime the question of economic coercion could not be left alone. The nonintercourse act was due to expire with the old Congress, and few were prepared to renew it. The damage it was doing to American commerce far exceeded the injury it was inflicting upon the European powers. France, for example, rather than tempering her actions, had stepped up her seizures of American vessels. To provide the United States with an escape from this dilemma, Nathaniel Macon, a veteran Republican from North Carolina (after consultation with and direction from Gallatin), introduced in Congress a bill, Macon's Bill No. 1. It would have permitted American ships to sail overseas and to import British and French goods, and it would have closed American ports to the public and private vessels of these two powers. Debate on the measure was protracted and bitter, revealing the new feelings that were emerging. For the first time members rose to suggest that there would be no relief from their burdens until Canada was taken. Representative Joseph Desha of Kentucky argued that no commercial measure could succeed so long as Britain held possessions "contiguous to the United States . . . ." All steps, he suggested, would be "unavailing while the British have Canada or a Nova Scotia on the Continent of America." He said, "You must remove the cause if you expect to perform the cure." He did not, he insisted, urge this step "because I think we want territory," but rather "because I think we need not calculate on a redress of grievances without the adoption of it, or something calculated to operate on the interests or fears of our enemies, for certainly we have seen enough to convince us that we have nothing to expect from their justice." Desha admitted that taking Canada would cost much "blood and treasure," but he argued that only in this way could the United States achieve "reparations for damages" and "secure commerce on reciprocal footings . . . ." [16]

In the Senate, Henry Clay advocated the same steps for the same reasons. He favored peace, he said, but he preferred "the troubled ocean of war demanded by the honor and independence

---

[16] *Annals of Congress,* 11th Congress, 1st and 2nd Sessions, II, 1306.

of the country . . . to the tranquil and putrescent pool of ignominious peace." If agreement could be reached with either Britain or France, he hoped it would be with Britain. But if no settlement could be attained with either, he wished for war with England, for she stood "prior in aggression," and was "pre-eminent in her outrage on us, by the violation of the sacred rights of American freemen, in the arbitrary and lawless impressment of our seamen, the attack on the *Chesapeake* . . . ." To those who argued that no object was attainable in such a war, he replied that Canada could be taken. Enormous advantages would flow from this. He declaimed:

Is it nothing to the pride of her monarch to have the last of the immense North American possessions held by him in the commencement of his reign wrested from his dominion? Is it nothing to us to extinguish the torch that lights up savage warfare? Is it nothing to acquire the entire fur trade connected with that country and to destroy the temptation and the opportunity of violating your revenue and other laws?[17]

This was not a speech, it should be said, revealing Clay's desire to go to war in order to annex Canada—although it has often been used as proof of this. It was, rather, an exposition of how Britain could best be fought. Clay was not the first to suggest the conquest of Canada, nor was he the last. And like all who proposed it, he was right. This was the only way that Britain could be challenged effectively, and as the operations of the war were to show, had the plan been implemented skillfully, it would have worked. After 1813 the balance of power in the interior shifted to America. Had her commanders not been so miserably incompetent in 1812 and had her army not been so totally unready, that shift might have taken place at the outset of the campaign, with fatal results for Britain.

Despite the forthright and belligerent speeches of Desha and Clay, not even Macon's original bill survived this Congress. It was passed in the House by a narrow margin but was emasculated in the Senate by an unholy combination of those who stood for stronger measures and those who favored no retalia-

---

[17] *Ibid.*, II, 580.

tion whatever. A substitute—Macon's Bill No. 2—was introduced and received Congressional approval in May 1810. This measure repealed the nonintercourse act of March 1809 and, startlingly enough, opened up, unrestricted commercial intercourse with the world. As an inducement to Britain and France to repeal their decrees, the bill authorized the President "in case either Great Britain or France, shall, before the 3d day of March next, so revoke or modify her edicts as that they shall cease to violate the neutral commerce of the United States" to apply nonimportation against whichever nation still refused to revoke her decrees.[18]

Again a belief in the effectiveness of economic pressure had triumphed. Again the United States held out a promise to side with one belligerent against the other as a bribe to gain the repeal of restrictive commercial systems. But of the several attempts at coercion, this was the least noble. Say what you will of the embargo, it had been conceived on a grand scale and was grounded on broad moral principles. The nonintercourse act had the merit of seeking to deprive those who injured the United States of American products. But Macon's Bill No. 2 merely threw American commerce open to those who had wrought the most injury upon the United States. It was an ignominious act of surrender. In the final analysis, it was submission to Britain, for she would benefit from the freeing of American commerce as France never could. Madison had few illusions about it. "However feeble it may appear," he wrote to Pinkney, "it is possible that one or the other of those powers may allow it more effect than was produced by the overtures heretofore tried." [19] This was the weapon which a distraught Congress produced to protect and uphold the national honor. Neither European belligerent was impressed, much less coerced by it. And why should either have been? But, it did provide Napoleon with an opportunity to embroil the United States even more bitterly and deeply with Britain.

Before Napoleon did this, however, the American govern-

---

[18] Quoted Henry Adams, *History of the United States during the Administration of Jefferson and Madison* (9 vols., New York, 1889–1891), V, 195.
[19] Madison to Pinkney, May 25, 1810, Hunt, *The Writings of James Madison*, VIII, 98.

ment made yet another attempt to settle her differences with Britain. As Jackson was no longer acceptable to Washington, the business was handled by Pinkney, the American minister in London. On November 13, 1809, Smith wrote him saying that the President wished the British government to recall Jackson immediately. This should be done, he said, in a manner that would leave no doubt of the "undiminished" desire of the United States to maintain relations with England on the "solid foundation of justice, of friendship, and of mutual interest." [20] This reasonable and courteous request met with a wholly unmerited delay—a delay that should have warned Pinkney that the new British government intended to be as rocklike in its resistance to America's demands as its predecessor. It was not until March 1810 that Wellesley returned an answer to the request. And although the reply was in the affirmative, it was couched in such fulsome praise for the disgraced minister that the United States might well have felt an additional affront. His Majesty, wrote Wellesley, was pleased to direct the return of Jackson, but he "has not marked, with any expression of his displeasure, the conduct of Mr. Jackson, whose integrity, zeal, and ability have long been distinguished in His Majesty's service . . . ." [21]

Pinkney's note concerning Jackson was followed by one dealing with the Orders in Council. A recent message from Armstrong, the American minister in Paris, had given to Pinkney what seemed to him the clue to the whole problem of Napoleon's decrees and Britain's edicts. Armstrong had asked in Paris what conditions would have to be fulfilled before the Berlin Decrees could be repealed. The Duc de Cadore had replied that the "only conditions required for the revocation . . . of the decree of Berlin will be a previous revocation by the British government of her blockade of France, or part of France (such as that from the Elbe to Brest, etc.), of a date anterior to that of the aforesaid decree." [22] Upon receiving this information, Pinkney set to work to determine what British blockades instituted before

---

[20] Smith to Pinkney, November 13, 1809, *American State Papers, Foreign Relations*, III, 323.

[21] Wellesley to Pinkney, March 14, 1810, *ibid.*, III, 355.

[22] Armstrong to Pinkney, January 10, 1810, *ibid.*, III, 350.

January 1, 1807, were still in force. He expected that Wellesley would tell him that "none of these blockades is in force," and he assumed then that such a declaration would "substantially" satisfy the French conditions. Instead, he was told that the coastline from Brest to the Elbe was blockaded in May 1806 and that this blockade was "comprehended in the order in council of the 7th January 1807 . . . ."[23] Nevertheless, Pinkney continued to hope that somehow Wellesley would conjure away the early blockade, and so set in motion a chain of events that would culminate in the repeal of the British Orders in Council and the French decrees. He was encouraged in his hope by Wellesley's manner, which was always one of great courtesy and friendliness. As Pinkney observed, "there was always an apparent anxiety on the part of Lord Wellesley to do what was conciliatory . . . ."[24] By April 1810, however, he began to suspect that his hopes were never to be fulfilled. He continued to press his case and to receive politeness but never a firm answer. In August he wrote bitterly of this "new" British practice of "returning no answer" to his flood of requests for information.[25]

Pinkney's efforts to settle the other issues with Britain were equally disappointing. In January 1810, Smith directed him to resume negotiations with the British government under full powers, which had been given jointly to him and Monroe. The old instructions of 1806 were revised, and two more conditions were added. First, before negotiations on a formal settlement could begin, the British must give satisfaction for the attack on the *Chesapeake;* and second, before a final treaty could be concluded, the Orders in Council would have to be repealed. As it was uncertain, when these instructions were drafted, what Congressional measures would be taken, Smith said that the President could not state categorically what precise conditions would be "annexed" to the repeal.[26] However, Pinkney was instructed to inform Britain that the President was disposed to put an end to the Congressional measures that had been

---

[23] Wellesley to Pinkney, March 2, 1810, *ibid.,* II, 350.

[24] Pinkney to Smith, March 21, 1810, *American State Papers, Foreign Relations,* III, 317.

[25] Pinkney to Smith, August 14, 1810, *ibid.,* III, 363.

[26] Smith to Pinkney, January 20, 1810, *ibid.,* III, 349.

THE SEARCH FOR ALTERNATIVES 71

enacted as a consequence of the Orders in Council and that he was equally disposed to maintain such measures against France if she persisted in retaining her decrees. Smith's instructions revealed a degree of optimism that did not comport with reality. It was vain to expect Pinkney to obtain in 1810 what he and Monroe had failed to secure in 1806. It was downright foolish to hope that he could, in addition, settle the *Chesapeake* affair and gain relief from the Orders in Council.

Nevertheless, Pinkney approached his task with determination and spirit. His early conversations with Wellesley raised his hopes, for the Foreign Secretary quickly agreed to terms on the *Chesapeake*. He raised no objections to returning the men seized from the American frigate, and he was prepared to offer suitable provisions for the families of the victims. Further, Wellesley was willing to forego any reference to the Presidential proclamation and to accept the proposal that the settlement include a statement that his government disavowed Admiral Berkeley's action and as a mark of its displeasure had removed him from his command. He would not agree to a trial and further punishment of the offending officer, but while this might have added frosting to the cake, it was not essential to an agreement.

Pinkney was justifiably elated. He had finally secured a highly favorable settlement on one of the most contentious issues in Anglo-American relations. And he had done it with speed and dispatch. But verbal agreement with Wellesley was one thing— a signed and sealed commitment was something else. Week followed week without the Foreign Secretary putting the treaty to paper. In July Pinkney wrote that he hoped the issue would soon "be brought to a conclusion," [27] but when nothing had been done by August, he was approaching a state of despair. He wrote:

I have found Wellesley upon every occasion given to procrastination beyond all example. The business of the *Chesapeake* is a striking instance. Nothing could be fairer than his conversations on that case. He settles it with me verbally over and over again. He promises his written overture in a few more days and I hear no more of the

---

[27] Pinkney to Smith, July 23, 1810, *ibid.*, III, 363.

matter. There may be cunning in all this, but it is not such cunning as I should expect from Lord Wellesley.[28]

Quite as irritating to Pinkney was Wellesley's extraordinary delay in appointing a new minister to Washington. The Foreign Secretary had informed Pinkney in July that it was his "intention immediately to recommend the appointment of an envoy extraordinary and minister plenipotentiary from the King to the United States." [29] By the beginning of August Pinkney wryly observed that he did not doubt that Wellesley "has long been looking out in *his dilatory way* for a suitable character (a man of rank) to send . . . to the United States." [30] At the end of the month he had received further assurances that a new minister would be appointed within two weeks and that the *Chesapeake* affair would be settled to America's satisfaction. But, said Pinkney, whose patience and trust were being exhausted, "There is no security that we shall have anything but promises. I am truly disgusted with this . . . ." [31]

His growing distrust of ever securing an agreement with Britain was shared by the President. Madison wrote:

Great Britain, indeed, may conceive that she has now a complete interest in perpetuating the actual state of things, which gives her the full enjoyment of our trade, and enables her to cut it off with every other part of the world; at the same time that it increases the chance of such resentment in France at the inequality as may lead to hostilities with the United States.

He drew some comfort from the possibility that "this very inequality which France would confirm by a state of hostilities with the United States, may become a motive with her to turn the tables on G. Britain by compelling her either to revoke her orders, or to lose the commerce of this country." [32] Smith held

---

[28] H. Wheaton, *Life, Writings and Speeches of William Pinkney* (New York, 1826), 447–448.

[29] Wellesley to Pinkney, July 22, 1810, *American State Papers, Foreign Relations*, III, 363.

[30] Wheaton, *Life, Writings and Speeches of William Pinkney*, 447.

[31] Pinkney to Smith, August 24, 1810, *American State Papers, Foreign Relations*, III, 366.

[32] Madison to Pinkney, May 23, 1810, Hunt, *The Writings of James Madison*, VIII, 98–99.

the same views as those of the President. He recognized that Macon's Bill worked in Britain's favor, and he suspected that London might be tempted to do nothing. But while admitting that Britain was under no pressure to change her policies, he felt that her refusal to do anything at all might have serious consequences. He suggested that France might comply with the terms of the bill, thus "retorting the inequality," or that the United States could, because of the "abuse of their amicable advances resume under new impressions, the subject of their foreign relations." [33]

America, however, did not re-examine her relations with Britain or take vigorous action against her at this time. If she had, she might have shaped events to her benefit. Further, America alone would have borne the responsibility for the action and would have paid the price for it with a clear conscience. But instead, as so often in the past, the administration hoped that others would relieve her distress. Previous experience should have taught Madison that this was unlikely, for nations seldom act out of a disinterested love of mankind. The events of 1810, when Napoleon gulled America into taking steps that were not justified by facts, proved how dangerous dependence on the good will or honesty of the warring powers could be. Any sudden shift in French policy should have been viewed with reservations, for Napoleon's attacks on American commerce had been long and willful. During the embargo, the Bayonne Decree had subjected American vessels to a sequestration, which was frequently accompanied by the imprisonment of their crews. The lifting of the embargo had not ended these seizures of goods and men, for France continued to find new excuses to justify such outrages. On March 23, 1810, the Rambouillet Decree (published in Paris on May 14, 1810) authorized the seizure and confiscation of all American vessels and their cargoes that had entered the ports of France, her colonies, or countries occupied by her. This act was made retroactive to May 20, 1809. The edict read that the decree was a consequence of the American nonintercourse act. But the widespread nature

---

[33] Smith to Pinkney, July 5, 1810, *American State Papers, Foreign Relations,* III, 362.

of the measure combined with the approaching sale of sequestered American property, with proceeds going to France,
showed its chief aim was looting, not retaliation.

The repeal of the nonintercourse act did not end the seizures.
The continuation of depredations by France enraged Madison.
Smith wrote Armstrong of the "high indignation" felt by the
"President as well as the public" over these acts of near piracy.
He warned that if there were an "absolute confiscation" of
American property, Washington could not consider applying
nonimportation to Britain.[34] A month later Smith wrote again
of the "enormity of the outrage" committed by France and the
"deep impressions" that so "signal an aggression" had made
upon the United States. He instructed Armstrong to convey
these views to Napoleon and to inform him that nonintercourse
would be applied to Britain only if "a satisfactory provision
for the property lately surprised and seized" were combined
with a "repeal of the French edicts." [35] Despite these continued
protests, Napoleon did nothing to diminish the pressures that
he was placing upon American commerce. Indeed, he increased
the scope of his aggression, for in August 1810 he signed a
secret decree ordering the sale of all sequestered American
merchandise and shipping. This decree, too, was made retroactive to the spring of 1809. This infamous measure, the effects
of which were soon felt, was not made known publicly until
1821 when Gallatin uncovered it. Angered by both its secrecy
and its purpose, he called it "a glaring act of combined injustice,
bad faith and manners . . . ." Further, he said, "no one can
suppose that if it had been communicated or published at the
same time the United States would, with respect to the promised
revocation of the Berlin and Milan Decrees, have taken that
ground which ultimately led to the war with Great Britain." [36]

Gallatin may well have been right in his assessment of what
would have happened had all America known of the Trianon
decree. Certainly the President, Congress, and the public were

---

[34] Smith to Armstrong, June 5, 1810, *ibid.*, III, 384.

[35] Smith to Armstrong, July 5, 1810, *ibid.*, III, 385.

[36] Gallatin to J. Q. Adams, September 15, 1821, H. Adams, *The Writings of
Albert Gallatin* (3 vols., Philadelphia, 1879), II, 197.

thoroughly aroused against France. And certainly Napoleon had given every evidence of supreme indifference to the reactions that his decrees had created. But suddenly when hostility was reaching the flash point in the United States, Napoleon reversed himself; instead of abusing America, he offered her what appeared to be the hand of friendship. In July 1810, Armstrong had given the Duc de Cadore unofficial notice of Macon's Bill No. 2. Although the immediate response to this was one of indifference, Napoleon had clearly decided to take advantage of the measure by August. At the beginning of that month, Cadore wrote to Armstrong:

. . . the decrees of Berlin and Milan are revoked, and . . . after the 1st of November they will cease to have effect; it being understood that, in consequence of this declaration, the English shall revoke their orders in council, and renounce the new principles of blockade which they have wished to establish; or that the United States, conformably to the act you have just communicated, shall cause their rights to be respected by the English.[37]

Here was a change indeed and one that was seized upon with precipitate speed by America. Nothing in Napoleon's career had shown a respect for the rights of neutrals, and any American administration faced with such an extraordinary reversal of policy should have approached it with the utmost caution and reserve. No action from Washington should have been taken until France's sincerity had been tested and her motives ascertained. The motives would not have been hard to uncover. It was always possible that Napoleon had become deeply concerned over the rising anti-French feeling in America. But this was as unlikely as Perceval suddenly repealing the order in council because they were annoying Washington. There were two major reasons for the Cadore letter. The first was that Napoleon saw a marvelous opportunity to further exacerbate Anglo-American relations. These were already stretched to the breaking point, and by inducing the United States to enforce nonintercourse against Britain they might be severed completely. The second and perhaps more important was that

---

[37] The Duke of Cadore to Armstrong, August 5, 1810, *American State Papers, Foreign Relations*, III, 367.

Europe desperately needed the American goods which were flowing overseas in such vast quantities. Macon's Bill had given relief to Britain but none to France. Why should Napoleon not try to reverse this? Jackson spoke of the huge number of vessels that were sailing to England but observed that "no shipments are made to France . . . ."[38] The movement of these goods was reflected in their prices which, Madison wrote, were falling "under a limitation of the market to G. Britain." "Cotton," he said, "is down at 10 or 11 cents in Georgia," and "the great mass of tobacco is in a similar situation."[39] To end this advantageous trade with Britain, then, was the aim of France. But the means used to achieve this had to be sophisticated. A simple and categorical repeal of the Berlin and Milan Decrees would result in the application of the nonintercourse act against Britain, but only if she failed to withdraw her Orders in Council. As Britain had always insisted that her decrees were made in retaliation to France's edicts, it seemed likely that a repeal of France's edicts would lead promptly to a withdrawal of Britain's Orders in Council. If both were withdrawn, trade with England would continue. To open American trade with France, but end it with Britain, required a measure sufficiently attractive for America but unacceptable to Britain. This was what the Cadore letter accomplished.

Instead of a straightforward renunciation of the Berlin and Milan Decrees, the Cadore letter made the repeal contingent upon two conditions—either of which would seriously injure Britain. The decrees would "cease to have effect," Cadore wrote, if the English "shall revoke their orders in council" and renounce their "new" principles of blockade; or if the United States should, in conformity to Macon's Bill, apply nonintercourse to Britain.[40] The first condition called for an act of faith as well as surrender. It would require faith if, without proof of the repeal of the French decrees, Britain were to give up her

---

[38] Jackson to Wellesley, July 10, 1810, F.O. 5:59.

[39] Madison to Jefferson, May 25, 1810, Hunt, *The Writings of James Madison*, VIII, 100.

[40] The Duke of Cadore to Armstrong, August 5, 1810, *American State Papers, Foreign Relations*, III, 386–387.

Orders in Council; and it would be surrender if, without proof of repeal, Britain were to renounce her blockades. It must be remembered that Napoleon defined a blockade as the investiture of a place by "land and sea."[41] Such a conception was totally unacceptable to Britain because it would vastly reduce the effectiveness of the Royal Navy. Thus military necessity alone made it more than likely that Britain would reject the Cadore letter. Other events in Europe confirmed Britain in the view that the repeal was a hoax. The Trianon decree was signed the very day that Cadore's letter was transmitted to Armstrong, and each passing month provided more evidence that American ships were being treated as fair prey. In the light of this no British government was going to alter its commercial policies. It would have been derelict in its duty if it had.

But if London received news of the Cadore letter with justified cynicism, what of America? She, too, recognized the conditional nature of the repeal. It was to take place some months in the future and only if one of two conditions obtained. Macon's Bill only provided for the application of nonintercourse ninety days after one or the other of the belligerents had revoked its decrees. Clearly the Cadore letter did not do this. Indeed, Armstrong was informed before he left Paris that the Berlin and Milan Decrees would remain in effect until November 1, and he was aware that a new schedule of French tariffs made the entrance of American goods into France chancy and difficult. Yet in spite of all this Madison decided to accept the letter at face value. On November 2 he issued a proclamation declaring that "the said edicts of France have been so revoked as they cease . . . to violate the neutral commerce of the United States," and that as a consequence nonintercourse would be applied to Britain on February if that country did not rescind her Orders in Council.[42]

Why did the President act as he did? He was aware of Napoleon's reputation for trickery and deceit. He himself had written two months before the Cadore letter that "with regard to the French government we are taught by experience to be . . .

---

[41] Champagny to Armstrong, August 22, 1809, *ibid.*, III, 325.
[42] J. D. Richardson, *A Compilation of the Messages and Papers of the Presidents 1789–1897* (20 vols., Washington, 1900), I, 482.

distrustful."[43] John Quincy Adams had no illusions about France. The Cadore letter, he wrote, held a "contingent snare to the United States," for if England rejected the offer "as France foresaw she would," the trap was laid that "would catch us in an English war." He continued by saying that "of the duplicity which prevailed in the French cabinet at that time I have had proofs that would give sight to the blind."[44] Three months later he warned that "Napoleon is ardently desirous of a war between the United States and England." He strongly urged that nonintercourse be applied "without hesitation and without delay to France," for she was continuing to enforce the Berlin and Milan Decrees.[45] Yet in spite of the widespread reservations held by many Americans and in spite of his own doubts concerning French reliability, Madison chose to enforce punitive legislation against Britain. Some have suggested that the President fell into a crude and clumsy trap. This may well be true. It is likely, however, that the President appreciated the dangerous course he was pursuing, but the accumulated frustrations and irritations he had suffered from Britain made him determined to use any weapon at hand. In May he wrote that "instead of an adjustment with either of the belligerents, there is an increased obstinacy in both . . . ." The inconveniences of nonintercourse had been exchanged, he complained, "for the greater sacrifices, as well as disgrace, resulting from a submission to the predatory systems."[46] This was particularly galling to the administration in Washington. All that Macon's bill had done was to open a roaring trade with Britain. As Britain had continually violated American interests, this increased trade was humiliating to the President and damaging to the pride and honor of his country. In June Madison wrote that although American opinion was outraged by France's "robberies," public attention was "beginning to fix itself on the proof [the cor-

---

[43] Madison to Pinkney, May 23, 1810, Hunt, *The Writings of James Madison*, VIII, 100.
[44] J. Q. Adams to Eustis, August 24, 1811, Ford, *The Writings of John Quincy Adams*, IV, 188.
[45] J. Q. Adams to T. B. Adams, November 6, 1811, *ibid.*, IV, 273–274.
[46] Madison to Pinkney, May 23, 1810, Hunt, *The Writings of James Madison*, VIII, 99.

respondence of Pinkney and Wellesley] it affords that the original sin agst. Neutrals lies with G.B. and that whilst she acknowledges it, she persists in it." [47] Three days before he actually issued the proclamation of November 2, he spoke of the "constant heartburning" on the subject of the *Chesapeake* and the "deep and settled indignation on the score of impressments, which can never be extinguished without a liberal atonement for the former and a systematic amendment of the latter." He added that the Cadore letter repealed the Berlin and Milan Decrees and that Wellesley's answers "discourage the hope that she [Britain] contemplates a reconciliation with us." [48]

Because he had become so disheartened over the possibility of securing redress from Britain and so discouraged at the prospects of gaining the repeal of the Orders in Council, Madison accepted the Cadore letter at face value. He could not coerce both powers, but perhaps he could pressure one at a time. He knew that his actions involved risks, but he was ready to accept them. In 1808 he had told Erskine that there was just cause for war with both Britain and France. By 1810 he had clearly become convinced that Britain's violations were the more oppressive and outrageous. The debate on the Macon bills showed that an increasing number of Congressmen shared this conviction. The Cadore letter might, as Adams suggested, be a trick to involve America in a war with Britain. But as Madison said, "We hope from the step, the advantage at least of having but one contest on our hands at a time." [49]

In February 1811, nonintercourse went into effect against Great Britain. This final step was the signal for a heated Congressional debate. Many members knew that Napoleon had seized American ships as late as December 1810—a knowledge that was hard to bear when Federalists stoutly declared that nonintercourse against Britain was unjust so long as France maintained the Berlin and Milan Decrees. Yet despite the disquieting news of continued French seizures and the failure by the new French minister, Sérurier, to deny the truth of

---

[47] Madison to Jefferson, June 22, 1810, *ibid.*, VIII, 103.
[48] Madison to Pinkney, October 30, 1810, *ibid.*, VIII, 120.
[49] Madison to Jefferson, October 19, 1810, *ibid.*, VIII, 109.

opposition allegations, Congressional Republicans were bound to support Madison. It was deemed necessary to introduce a bill to enforce nonintercourse against Britain, since some feared that the courts might rule that the Cadore letter was not sufficient proof of the repeal of the French edicts and that the Presidential proclamation was therefore invalid. But the measure placed before Congress was less stringent than Macon's Bill No. 2 envisaged; it only provided for the nonimportation of British goods. This mildness was not the result of qualms of conscience but rather of Americans' desire to export goods to the United Kingdom. Thus Macon's halfhearted measure was further weakened by a Congress that put private profit above public interest.

Congressional exchanges on this bill were harsh and bitter. Some opponents of the President laid bare the precarious grounds upon which he had acted, and others demanded the defeat of the bill itself. Its defeat was of course impossible for it would have left Madison exposed to unbearable public humiliation. So the bill was passed, and the United States was committed to a course of action that would lead to further collisions with Britain. That justification existed for the government's action cannot be denied. The pity of it was that the President rested his defense upon a demonstrable falsehood. And worse, he clung to it through thick and thin. The shaping of foreign policy is a delicate business in which timing and judgment are vital factors. Madison's timing may have been adequate, but his judgment was faulty, for he continually insisted publicly that the Berlin and Milan Decrees had been repealed and consequently his government's measures were justifiable. This stubborn refusal to admit error gave comfort to his opponents at home and confirmed the British in their view that they were dealing with a weak and unstable government. No great power is likely to make concessions under these circumstances.

But if the President lacked acute judgment, Congress was not much better. It was quite clear that the nonintercourse act raised the possibility of war with Britain. Yet the legislature did nothing to arm the country against the event. It abandoned a bill to raise a force of 50,000 troops, and it abolished the

Bank of the United States. The 50,000 troops would have been the minimum needed to defend the nation, and the Bank was essential to the health of the economy. Further, Congress refused to raise the taxes to compensate the treasury for the loss of income that would follow the enforcement of the nonintercourse act. Only for the navy was any action taken, but here the appropriations were so parsimonious as to make the gesture meaningless. The inadequacies of military preparations are doubly puzzling when it is remembered that in the autumn of 1810 the President had given orders to occupy the West Floridas. This was a step which, though unlikely, could have led to war with Spain. Yet even this possibility did not stir the Eleventh Congress into taking the measures demanded by the circumstances. The explanation for this somnolent behavior lay in the fact that a majority did not want to contemplate war, while the aggressive minority that did had an unrealistic appreciation of what fighting involved. Clay had proclaimed, "I verily believe that the militia of Kentucky are alone competent to place Montreal and Upper Canada at your feet." [50] This opinion, as Erskine observed, was widely held. Too few people recognized that war was a tough business. Most comforted themselves with the thought that, if it came, the battle would be swift and short and the victory sweet. This illusion exists too frequently when the smell of war is in the air, and it is almost always dispelled by the hard reality of military operations.

America would have been better served if heady talk of fighting had been replaced by a cold analysis of the situation. It was a situation bad enough to give pause to the most enthusiastic, for relations with Britain were deteriorating at an accelerating rate. The introduction of nonintercourse coincided very nearly with the departure of Pinkney from London. The American minister had striven long, hard, and fruitlessly to secure an accommodation with Britain. He had begun with the *Chesapeake* affair and continued by pressing for the appointment of a minister to replace Jackson in Washington. His efforts had been received with courtesy and procrastination. The

---

[50] *Annals of Congress*, 11th Congress, 1st and 2nd Sessions, 1, 580.

appearance of the Cadore letter burdened him with an even heavier task, for it was now his duty to persuade England to withdraw her Orders in Council. On October 19 he was instructed to inform Britain of the penalties that would be imposed upon her if she remained intransigent. He was also told that he should attempt to settle impressment—a practice to which the Secretary of State said, "no nation can submit consistently with its independence." [51]

If Pinkney's instructions had been difficult before, they were now little short of impossible. It was absurd to expect Britain to end impressment. It was equally unrealistic to expect her to lift the Orders in Council when all the evidence showed that Napoleon had not rescinded his decrees. Yet Pinkney had his orders, and he followed them clearly and consistently as any public servant should. However, he must at times have wondered at the quality of the mind that produced them. In November he wrote the Foreign Secretary that the United States had a "right to expect upon every principle of justice" a revocation of the Orders in Council.[52] As might be expected, he received no immediate answer, for Wellesley had elevated procrastination to the level of high art. After a month had passed, Pinkney rightly concluded that, on the Orders in Council, London would do "nothing if they can help it." [53] When he finally received an answer at the end of the year, it confirmed his earlier expectations. Wellesley exposed the conditional nature of Napoleon's actions but added that if Pinkney could provide proof of an "absolute" repeal of the decrees, Britain would be pleased to revoke her Orders in Council.[54] In a lengthy reply the American minister attempted to answer Wellesley's charges. But he knew how difficult it was to do this effectively and he was certain of the hopelessness of his case. This was shown in the concluding paragraph of his letter in which he said that he was not in possession of "any documents which you are likely

---

[51] Smith to Pinkney, October 19, 1810, *American State Papers, Foreign Relations*, III, 370.

[52] Pinkney to Wellesley, November 3, 1810, *ibid.*, III, 373.

[53] Pinkney to Smith, December 14, 1810, *ibid.*, III, 173.

[54] Wellesley to Pinkney, December 29, 1810, *ibid.*, III, 409.

to consider as authentic" proof of the repeal.[55] The same day he sent a note to Wellesley stating that, because the British government was still represented in Washington by only a chargé d'affaires, the United States could no longer be represented in London by a minister plenipotentiary. He wished, therefore, to have an official audience so that he might take leave of the country. This meeting was granted in February, and America was left without a minister in Britain until the War of 1812 was over.

Although his official reason for leaving was the failure of Wellesley to replace Jackson in Washington, the real motive for Pinkney's departure was his conviction that he could no longer serve his country. He had ruefully concluded that Britain did not want a settlement. Wellesley had, he said, "inadvertently" remarked to him that it was the opinion of many people that "the *British interest in America* would be completely destroyed by sending at this time a Minister Plenipotentiary" to Washington. There was, Pinkney observed, "cunning at the bottom" of this.[56] The American minister had once thought that sheer inertia explained Wellesley's behavior. He now believed that Britain simply did not want to change the situation. And he was right. The Orders in Council, blockades, and impressment were vital parts of Britain's armory. She would not surrender them until either Napoleon was defeated or they no longer served England's purpose. That moment had not yet arrived, and Pinkney knew it. And so he left. For nearly five years he had pressed America's case with dedication and perseverance. He had served under two presidents and had been unable to secure a tenth of what they had wanted. His inability to fulfill their wishes should not be construed as a reflection on his talents, but rather should be seen as the result of a British policy so inflexible that no one man could alter it.

A short time after Pinkney left London, the Eleventh Congress expired. It, too, had hoped to wring concessions from Britain, but it had ended with Macon's Bill No. 2 and then, in desperation, the nonintercourse act. It was not a record to be proud

---

[55] Pinkney to Wellesley, January 14, 1811, *ibid.*, III, 409.
[56] Wheaton, *Life, Writings and Speeches of William Pinkney,* 454.

of. Admittedly the problems it faced were enormously difficult, and admittedly few of its members wanted war. But Congress should have taken steps to arm the country for the future. Instead, Congress wrangled and debated but did nothing. With firmer presidential direction it might have accomplished more. But the frustrations of Pinkney and Congress were reflections of the frustrations of the President. Continuous negotiations had failed to improve America's position. And yet because of his country's weakness, Madison feared to contemplate war. This dilemma accounts for his use of the Cadore letter and for his wriggling from one expedient to another. But time was running out, and Madison knew that he would soon have to make hard decisions. What confronted the President also faced the country as a whole. A new Congress had been elected and was to convene in the autumn of 1811. Its leaders had tired of barren talks and wanted to take forceful measures without counting the cost.

CHAPTER IV

War as a Final Solution

A NEW ERA OF TURBULENCE was ushered in with the new Congress. It faced a world in which there was no relief in sight from the strains and stresses in foreign policy. Indeed, these became worse as further incidents on the high seas inflamed American tempers. The domestic scene was harsher too, for there was widespread economic trouble in the country, and most people ascribed it to the policies that Britain was pursuing overseas. To cap it all, a series of dangerous crises blew up in the interior. Again many Americans believed that these crises were directly attributable to British intrigue. It is little wonder that both the President and Congress became more belligerent in word and deed. It was, of course, not too late for Britain to relieve these pressures and save the situation. But necessity had wedded the government of Perceval to the maritime practices that were deepening the gulf between the two countries. Macon's Bill No. 2 had merely confirmed the Tories in their conviction that stern measures would bend America to Britain's will. In any event, few in England liked America; imperial powers seldom love those who have thrown off their control through revolution. Then, too, many believed that the United States was pro-French. This charge against Jefferson and Madison was hardly fair, but in war those who are not with you are thought to be against you. There were, of course, moderate men in Britain who favored concessions to America, but they were not yet powerful enough to force the government to alter its policies. They began to grow in strength, however, in 1811, as a depression settled upon parts of England's economy. As their protests increased, the government was finally persuaded to repeal the Orders in Council. But this concession came too late to prevent war.

The Twelfth Congress, which took office in the fall of 1811, faced America's problems with more vigor and a clearer sense of direction than had its predecessors. This is not to say that it was united in its views or that it consistently pursued a clear and coherent policy. It was frequently divided over issues and at odds with itself. Yet within it there existed a group of men who did want to take a strong line and were prepared to cajole and drive their colleagues toward the goals they sought. Some of these men had served in the previous Congress, but their ranks had swelled in the recent election. Because national parties were more fluid and party allegiance less binding then than now, it is difficult to generalize about the structure of Congress in 1811. There was a greater ebb and flow in the Twelfth Congress than in current ones. Further, the election itself was not fought on the clear-cut issue of peace or war. Had the Presidency been contested, there might have been greater clarification of national opinion. But the issues in off-year elections are often regional in nature and personal in character. As a consequence, in some areas foreign policy and trade were important, but in others the personality of the candidate and interparty squabbles were determining factors.

Nevertheless, this Congress was different from its predecessors, for it contained the men who made a declaration of war possible. Some have suggested that its drive and energy were due to the high proportion of young members. Henry Clay of Kentucky and Felix Grundy of Tennessee were thirty-four, while John C. Calhoun was only twenty-nine. John A. Harper of New Hampshire was thirty-two, and Peter B. Porter of New York thirty-eight. These were young men, but their youth was offset by the age of senior members, including several octogenarians. In fact, the average age of the Twelfth Congress was roughly the same as that of the Eleventh. If it was not age that accounted for the differences between the two Congresses, perhaps it was the number of new members in the Twelfth. The defeat of a high percentage of the old representatives was called by Robert Wright of Maryland "the sentence of the nation against the doctrine of submission." [1] There were some states where remarkable shifts took place. New Hampshire elected a completely new slate of candidates. There were pronounced shifts in the delegations from Pennsylvania, New York, Massachusetts, Maryland, Virginia, New Jersey, and North Carolina. Of the states with sizable representation, only Connecticut showed virtually no change. Many of these shifts resulted from local circumstances. The personality of the individual and the state of party efficiency influenced the outcome of many of these contests. But large turnovers had been witnessed before. The Eleventh Congress had seen changes of nearly the same magnitude. And yet the significance of the election of the Twelfth Congress cannot be ignored. It returned some 106 Republicans (many of them with strong and aggressive views) and only 36 Federalists.

What really distinguished the new Congress was the quality of the men in it who were reaching for power. Neither youth nor age is the real test of ability. What matters is whether a man has the knowledge of what should be done and the skill and determination to see things through to the end. The War Hawks had these qualities. They did not remember the Revolution; most of them had been born either just before or during it. They lacked the caution of those who had fought and won that war and now wanted to rest rather than risk the results of victory in another battle. Jefferson spoke for the older group when he wrote to Langdon, "I think one war enough for the life of one man: and you and I have gone through one which at least may lessen our impatience to embark in another." [2] But Clay and his followers had no patience with this kind of caution and restraint. They were representative of a new breed of nationalists. Although they were less violent and more mature than the men who emerge in many countries under similar circumstances, they were still politicians who wanted

---

[1] Quoted Irving Brant, *James Madison, The President 1809–1812* (New York, 1956), 379.
[2] Jefferson to Langdon, August 2, 1808, Paul L. Ford (ed.), *The Writings of Thomas Jefferson* (10 vols., New York, 1892–1899), XI, 40.

action and strong action, and they were prepared to force their way into the seats of power to achieve it.

The contests for the Senate were less significant than those for the House, for only one third of its members were up for re-election. Yet there were some important changes. Timothy Pickering, a Federalist of long standing from Massachusetts, lost his seat. He was the man who had once proposed the toast: "The World's last hope—Britain's fast anchored Isle." His replacement, the Republican Joseph Varnum, brought less ability to the Senate, but he could at least generally be counted on to support the President. Both Kentucky and Tennessee returned Republicans, George Bibb and George Campbell; William Giles was re-elected in Virginia. The results left the Senate in the hands of Madison's party by a ratio of roughly three to one. Although many of these Republicans were not members of the war party in 1811, circumstances were to drive some of the uncommitted into the arms of Clay and his supporters.

As Congress began to reflect the new forces in the country, Madison took steps to improve his cabinet. After months of inaction, he finally decided to rid himself of his Secretary of State. For too long he had put up with Smith who had little perception and less talent. The Secretary hardly knew how to draw up instructions for his assistants, and he lacked a clear idea of where his country should go or how it should act. Even worse, he was not committed to the President. He was privately critical of the administration, and he sponsored attacks upon it. He quarreled with men of greater ability and intrigued with the small minds with which he surrounded himself. Incompetence in high office is hard to bear, but combined with disloyalty it is intolerable. A final dispute with Gallatin forced Madison's hand, and he decided to remove Smith from office. He offered him the embassy in St. Petersburg, but Smith, whose reach exceeded his grasp, wanted London. The President had no intention of placing the most important foreign post in the hands of such a mischief-maker and told him so. Smith then resigned his office and issued a violent broadside charging the President with following policies that were unwise and unworkable. As a successor, Madison chose Monroe who had just become governor of Virginia. Monroe was interested in the offer but disturbed lest his sudden departure from Virginia be considered a betrayal of the high state office. Of even greater concern to him was his deep consciousness of the differences he had had in the past with both Jefferson and Madison. He had always felt that the treaty he and Pinkney had negotiated with England should have been accepted, and he still believed that it was imperative to work out an accommodation with this "great maritime power, even on moderate terms, rather than hazard war, or any other alternative." [3] Upon being assured that this was the President's hope, he decided to accept the cabinet post. He did so in the belief that he could give direction to his country's foreign policy, heal the divisions within his party, and advance his own political fortunes.

But if Monroe felt that his previous service in Britain would make his relations with that country easier, he was in for a rude shock. The old problems remained, but in an exaggerated and more acute form, and there were new ones. He was forced to conduct futile and ritualistic negotiations over the Orders in Council, and he was compelled to deal with another crisis over impressment. This issue had lain dormant for many months while the government wrestled with other problems. Matters like the Cadore letter, Macon's bills, and the debate over non-intercourse were exercising the minds of politicians. However, impressment still lay close to the surface, and any flagrant incident could bring it back to the forefront with a vengeance. In 1811 this happened. For some months British ships had been brazenly impressing sailors off the American coast. American tempers, already short, exploded when *HMS Guerrière* seized an American citizen from a coasting vessel off Sandy Hook. A prompt demand was made to John Morier, the British chargé in Washington, that the impressed sailor be returned immediately. Morier was surprised and disturbed at the heat generated by the incident. He wrote Wellesley:

. . . from the Circumstances of this Impressment having taken place on board of a coasting vessel; a greater degree of Indignation has been

---

[3] Monroe to Madison, March 23, 1811, S. M. Hamilton, *The Writings of James Monroe* (7 vols., New York, 1898–1903), V, 182.

raised against us than usual in the ordinary Cases of this nature and
the Government, whose Popularity was diminishing fast . . . have no
doubt made the best use of this as a fresh Proof of Aggression on our
Part to justify their Principles of Opposition to Great Britain.[4]

In a note to Rear Admiral Herbert Sawyer, he urged the
speedy return of the seaman for reasons of "Justice and of
Policy"—justice because the seizure was made in American
coastal waters and policy because the incident had so aroused
the public. The subject of impressment, he observed,

. . . has always been one by which the popular Feeling of this Nation
has been kept alive in its Animosity against Great Britain . . . . I am
confident that no possible advantage which can accrue to the Service
even if five hundred Men were annually procured in that way, can
compensate for the Evil which a constant State of Irritation between
the two Nations must create.[5]

The dangers that Morier feared were dramatically realized
in the tragic clash between the *President* and the *Little Belt*.
The *President*, an American frigate, was one of a squadron
ordered to protect vessels from molestation within territorial
waters. In 1810, Commodore John Rodgers, the commanding
officer of the squadron, had issued instructions to his subordinates "to maintain and support at every risk and cost the dignity
of our flag" and to return with interest any fire aimed in their
direction.[6] The stage had been set for a confrontation, and
the actions of the *Guerrière* triggered it. Shortly after the news
of the impressment by the *Guerrière* reached Annapolis, Morier
wrote that the *President* had sailed with instructions "to take
the Man by Force, from the British frigate if he was not delivered up." [7] In this particular the British chargé was mistaken,
although the rage expressed by public officials was so great
that he, as well as many Americans, believed that such orders
had actually been issued. On May 16 the *President* was some

---

[4] Morier to Wellesley, No. 25, June 4, 1811, F.O. 5:74.

[5] Morier to Sawyer, May 20, 1811, F.O. 5:74.

[6] Rodgers to Secretary of Navy, August 4, 1810, Captain's Letters, quoted
A. T. Mahan, *Sea Power in its Relation to the War of 1812* (2 vols., London,
1905), I, 257.

[7] Morier to Sawyer, May 20, 1811, F.O. 5:74.

fifty miles off Cape Henry when a sail was seen bearing down upon her. The vessel in sight was the corvette *Little Belt*, commanded by Captain Bingham. She had just come from Bermuda and was in search of the *Guerrière* which she was to join. Upon closing with the American frigate, Bingham saw that she was not the ship he sought and so sheared off, resuming his previous course. The *President*, thinking that she was the *Guerrière*, promptly gave chase and finally caught up with her at nightfall. Precisely what happened next has never been determined, for the evidence of one ship's company flatly contradicts that of the other. Apparently each vessel simultaneously hailed the other, then exchanged single shots, and finally full broadsides. The *President*, a frigate with a far heavier weight of metal than a corvette, soon silenced the *Little Belt*, killing nine and wounding twenty-three of her crew. Payment for the *Chesapeake* had finally been exacted. Toasts were drunk in America celebrating the event and newspapers proclaimed a victory for righteousness backed by force. In England fears were expressed that the United States would be so elated with its victory that the Americans would be increasingly difficult to deal with.

In the midst of this high drama the new British minister, Augustus John Foster, arrived in America. He had been appointed by Wellesley, but too late to prevent Pinkney's departure from London. He was young, personable, and well connected. And he was not without diplomatic experience, for he had served in Washington under Merry and latterly as chargé in Stockholm. But these qualities did not outweigh his shortcomings. As so many Englishmen of his background and education, he found much to dislike in the United States. Washington, he admitted, was the most agreeable of any American city to live in, but it still fell short of most civilized places. American manners were, as expected, crude, and most people lacked refinement. He was amused by the breaches of taste that he saw around him, and he was condescending toward the majority of those who came in touch with him. Given these attitudes, it was unlikely that he would be able to succeed where others had failed. What was needed in Washington was a man of great skill and perception, but in the tense state of Anglo-

American relations even such a diplomat would probably have failed. Unfortunately, Britain did not consider America important enough to warrant a diplomat of this caliber. A heavy price was exacted for making such a foolish and rudimentary mistake in judgment.

Like those before him Foster faced a multitude of problems, and like his predecessors he was limited by his instructions in the actions he could take. He was to offer a settlement of the *Chesapeake* affair. This, fortunately, was to be the least difficult task he faced, although its resolution was delayed by the clash between the *President* and the *Little Belt*. He then was to deal with the Orders in Council. The British government did not contemplate their repeal under present circumstances, and Foster was authorized to repeat the usual arguments that the French repeal was conditional and therefore did not justify the steps that America had taken. The question of Fox's blockade was also involved here, for Madison had insisted that paper blockades be lifted simultaneously with the Orders in Council. Britain was prepared to meet the United States halfway on this issue, however. If she maintained such blockades, it would only be under accepted terms of international law. But if the United States insisted upon a French definition of a blockade—that a place had to be invested by sea and land—there would be trouble, for Britain would never accept it. Finally, Foster was to register two protests—one against the use of American ports by French privateers and the other against the occupation of West Florida, which Wellesley characterized as an act "contrary to every principle of public Justice, faith and National Honor, and so injurious to the alliance, subsisting between His Majesty and the Spanish Nation." [8]

The last two points were quickly adjusted. Monroe insisted that he was quite unaware of any French privateers using the ports of the United States. And because Morier said that he knew of none either, Foster dropped the matter. The occupation of West Florida, the British minister informed Monroe, was considered by his government as an act of aggression. He was curtly told that the President had taken the step in order to

---

[8] Wellesley to Foster, No. 3, April 20, 1811, F.O. 5:75.

defend the "rights" and secure the "peace" of America.[9] As Foster had neither the authority nor the desire to pursue the matter any further, it too was shelved. More success met his efforts to settle the *Chesapeake* affair. Foster offered a disavowal of Berkeley's actions, the return of those taken from the American frigate, and compensation to the victims and their families. These terms were agreeable to Monroe, but the problem of the *President* and the *Little Belt* had first to be disposed of. Foster insisted that before he sign a settlement of the *Chesapeake* he receive a satisfactory explanation of the "wanton slaughter" of British subjects aboard the *Little Belt*.[10] Monroe would have none of this. The fault lay with the British corvette, he replied, and in any event reparation for a prior damage should be made before atonement for a subsequent incident could be considered. Foster felt compelled to postpone talks; he wrote in a baffled tone to Wellesley that the Secretary of State "showed very little concern about the proposed settlement . . . ."[11] He should not have been so puzzled, for America had waited so long for an honorable settlement that she was becoming mightily bored with the whole matter.

A way out of this impasse was presented to Foster when an American court of inquiry was held to determine responsibility for the clash between the *President* and the *Little Belt*. The court found the British ship responsible for the conflict, and while this was not the result Foster had hoped for, he nevertheless felt that Washington's actions had fulfilled Britain's demand for an investigation of the incident. He therefore renewed his offer. In November Madison accepted the terms, saying that it was regrettable that reparation "should have been so long delayed . . . ."[12] And indeed it was. Jefferson's insistence upon linking impressment to compensation had delayed talks in the beginning. But once these two issues had been separated, the dilatory conduct of Britain had held up a settle-

---

[9] Monroe to Foster, July 8, 1811, *American State Papers, Class I, Foreign Relations*, III, 543.

[10] Foster to Wellesley, No. 7, July 18, 1811, F.O. 5:76.

[11] Foster to Wellesley, No. 7, July 18, 1811, F.O. 5:76.

[12] Monroe to Foster, November 12, 1811, *American State Papers, Foreign Relations*, III, 500.

ment. This delay was doubly unfortunate. When graciously offered reparations would have silenced American criticism and healed a breach in her relations with Britain, they were inexcusably withheld. When the reparations could no longer stop the rapid descent of both countries toward war, they were reluctantly granted. As Madison wrote, the compensation takes "a splinter out of our wounds; but besides the provoking tardiness of the remedy, the moment finally chosen deprives it of much of its effect, by giving it the appearance of a mere anodyne to the excitement in Congs. and the nation produced by the contemporary disclosures." [13]

The discussions on the Orders in Council were protracted and unavailing. Foster put Wellesley's position to Monroe with little result. The propositions that the French repeal was conditional, that it was untrue, that French municipal regulations were accomplishing the same purpose as the Berlin and Milan Decrees, and that Britain could not repeal her edicts in the light of these circumstances left Monroe unmoved. Beyond these familiar arguments Britain had little to offer. Foster was able to say that his country would reverse an earlier condemnation of a number of American ships recently captured. These vessels had sailed from the United States believing that the Cadore letter would lead Britain to lift her Orders in Council. This last concession proved to be short-lived, however, for the British cabinet did an about-face on the subject within a month. Worse, this action was soon followed by new threats against America. If the United States persisted in her actions against Britain, Wellesley told Foster, he was to remind Monroe that Britain could "resort to adequate means of retaliation." [14] America should be reminded of the extensive means by which Britain could affect her commerce without "resorting to the extremity of war." None of this was sufficient to influence Madison and Monroe. The President was committed to a course of action based upon the acceptance of the Cadore letter, and

[13] Madison to J. Q. Adams, November 15, 1811, Gaillard Hunt, *The Writings of James Madison* (7 vols., New York, 1900–1910), VIII, 167.

[14] Wellesley to Foster, No. 8, secret, April 1811, B. Mayo, *Instructions to the British Ministers to the United States 1791–1812* (Washington, 1941), 324.

nothing would budge him from it. Monroe did suggest that a revocation of the Orders in Council, couched in the same kind of language as the French repeal, might be satisfactory to Washington, but Foster did not grasp at the opportunity offered him. It is doubtful that events would have been different if he had, for his government's position was inflexible. Britain would not change until given clear and unalterable proof that Napoleon had altered his attitude. Indeed, Britain had now gone further, for Perceval wanted not only a repeal of the Berlin and Milan Decrees but also an assurance that British goods would have free access to Europe. France would never agree to this. Foster's task was, therefore, nearly impossible of fulfillment. "No argument," he wrote, "no mode of reasoning . . . can avail in a discussion with such tempers . . . ." [15] Monroe might, with justice, have replied in kind.

It was clear that America and Britain had reached a deadlock. Each passing week provided more evidence of the seriousness of this impasse. In July Foster was informed that the United States was prepared to settle "every other difference" with England if the "Orders in Council are revoked . . . ." [16] He was also told that "if the United States should find it necessary to extend the Non importation act to France, it is not the intention of the President to remove its operation as it respects Great Britain unless His Majesty's Orders are revoked." [17] In November he was informed that the "honour" of the United States forced her to apply nonimportation against Britain, and he was chided for the "impolicy" of not seizing upon the Cadore letter as the pretext for "revoking the Orders in Council . . . ." [18] He was even told that no minister would be appointed to London until the Orders in Council were repealed, for even if the President nominated an individual for the post, the Senate would refuse to confirm him. The weight of this evidence convinced Foster that only Britain could break the log jam. It would be worthwhile, he wrote home, to repeal the Orders in

---

[15] Foster to Wellesley, No. 5, July 7, 1811, F.O. 5:76.

[16] Foster to Wellesley, No. 7, July 18, 1811, F.O. 5:76.

[17] Foster to Wellesley, No. 8, July 18, 1811, F.O. 5:76.

[18] Foster to Wellesley, No. 22, November 9, 1811, F.O. 5:77.

Council—at least as far as the United States was concerned.
If this were not done, he said, the worst would come. The
American people, he reported, were tired of their present pre-
dicament and would prefer "a state of War rather than a
continuance of their present embarrassments." [19] Further talks
with Madison confirmed him in this view. The United States,
he suggested, is "so tied down to the line of conduct they have
taken that they cannot give it up without absolute dishonour,
and yet are so reduced by the wasting policy they have pursued
as to be anxious to catch at some plea for ending it, the only
alternative now left them being the ruinous one of war." [20]

Congress assembled in November 1811, and it soon gave
confirmation to Foster's opinions. Its sessions provided a sound-
ing board for all the bitter complaints that were being leveled at
Britain. They were many and events had conspired to produce
more; besides the old familiar ones about neutral rights, trade,
and the Orders in Council, there were the more recent ones concerning Indian trouble on the frontier and economic distress
in the Mississippi Valley. Both of these problems were attributed
to the British, and both aroused the anger of militant nationalists from the South and the West.

The problem of the interior was one of long standing. Indeed, it predated the Revolution and had a cyclical quality as
its intensity rose and fell with the rhythm of westward expansion. After the Treaty of 1783 the interior posed particular
difficulties in the United States, for Britain held on to Western
posts that she should have transferred to America. Her motives
for retaining them in violation of the treaty were mixed, but
the most important one was the desire to placate the Indians
who had been betrayed in the negotiations leading to the peace.
The real danger of an Anglo-American conflict over this issue
was removed in 1794 with Jay's Treaty. But although one problem was resolved, others were not. The expansion of white
settlers into Indian territory too frequently brought bloodshed.
Treaties made by Washington were often misunderstood by
the Indians and broken by the whites. Deception, dishonest

---

[19] Foster to Wellesley, No. 26, November 23, 1811, F.O. 5:77.
[20] Foster to Wellesley, No. 29, November 29, 1811, F.O. 5:77.

trading, and plunder of the land worked to create distrust between the two races. Pushed ever westward by a seemingly inexhaustible stream of insatiably hungry settlers, it is little wonder that the Indians looked to the north for support.

It was at this point that the problem became international, not domestic, and that the role played by Britain became of vital concern to America. The United States often misunderstood British motives and invariably distrusted them. There was, unhappily, room for misunderstanding. After the Treaty of Grenville in 1795 and the evacuation of the posts in 1796, Britain began the process of severing her relations with the Indians. Peace had presumably settled upon the frontier, and there was no point in continuing the grants of assistance to the tribes. The *Chesapeake* incident changed all this, for British North America now faced the imminent possibility of an invasion from the United States. Consequently, the British in Canada began to cultivate the Indians once again. But this time it was a clear case of cause and effect. It was the fear of an American attack that moved Britain to go to the Indians. She did not work for closer ties with them in order to incite trouble with the United States.

Britain's new policy bristled with difficulties. Officials in Canada had to encourage the Indians to ally themselves with Britain and to convince them that in event of war the various tribes should give military aid to the Crown. Yet while arousing interest and support, they had to exert restraint to dampen their ardor lest the tribes launch the first attack. To implement this policy, the British invited Shawnee chiefs from Ohio to Amherstburg where British agents elaborated on the theme of American duplicity and offered the Indians the hand of friendship. Even Tecumseh joined the trek north. So successful were these overtures that by 1810 Mathew Elliot, the Indian agent at Amherstburg, was convinced that Britain could, with the help of the tribes, control the territory between Detroit and the Ohio.

Although many Americans were concerned over this increased activity on their frontier, few strongly denounced it in the beginning. Representatives from both the maritime and interior states concentrated their fire, instead, on the violation of neutral rights. By 1811, however, all this began to change. British policy had been too successful. The offer of support to the Indians had done more than restore friendly relations: it had made the Indians ready and eager for war. Unfortunately, continued American expansion was soon to give them the excuse for precipitate action. This potential for disaster frightened Sir James Craig, the Governor-in-Chief of Canada. Indian support in the event of a future conflict was one thing; a war initiated by them was another. Everyone realized that a conflict in the interior could cause an explosion whose reverberations would be felt overseas. Therefore Craig set out to check the process that he had started. In February 1811, he wrote Francis Gore, Lieutenant Governor of Upper Canada, that it was to Britain's interest to "prevent a rupture between the Indians, and the subjects of the United States." Conveniently, he said, he had ordered all officers in the Indian Department "to use all their influence to dissuade the Indians from their projected plan of hostility, giving them clearly to understand, that they must not expect any assistance from us." Such a policy of dissuasion must be pursued, he continued, because an Indian war "would expose us to a continual state of suspicion and irritation on the part of the Americans which sooner or later, would probably lead us into being ourselves parties in the war, however much we might wish to avoid it." [21] Craig's policy was London's policy; when Craig returned to that city in the summer of 1811, instructions were issued to his *locum tenens* to continue it.

When Sir George Prevost arrived in Quebec in September 1811, to take over the reins of government, he found that the situation on the frontier was rapidly deteriorating because of mounting Indian hostility and increasing American bellicosity. This situation reached a climax on November 7 when Governor William Henry Harrison of Indiana Territory fought the battle of Tippecanoe. The responsibility for this affair rests on the shoulders of an officer whose zeal exceeded his good sense, but the dangers he saw developing on the frontier moved him to

---

[21] *Michigan Pioneer and Historical Collections* (40 vols., Lansing, Michigan, 1877–1929), XXV, 280–281.

act as he did. Tecumseh, the chief of the Shawnees, and his brother, the Prophet, were attempting to unite the tribes of the Mississippi Valley into a confederacy that would drive the whites out of the Northwest and make that area an Indian preserve. The headquarters for this movement was at a village on Tippecanoe Creek where it flowed into the Wabash River. Choosing a moment when Tecumseh was visiting the South, Harrison collected a force of regular troops and volunteers, marched into the heart of the Prophet's country, and camped outside his village. Faced with a direct threat to their security, the Indians fell upon the American army. In the ensuing battle Harrison broke the attack, destroyed the Indian village, and then retired. But the mischief had been done. Efforts by the British to control the Indians now seemed doomed to failure. In December 1811, General Isaac Brock reported that "such was their infatuation the Indians refused to listen to advice . . . ." Indeed, they had become so involved in their war that he despaired "of being able to withdraw them from the contest in time to avert their destruction, a high degree of fanaticism which has been for years working in their minds has led to the present state of things." [22]

Yet because Britain did not want a local conflagration to get out of hand, she still tried to restrain the Indians. It was a difficult business to manage, and in trying to arrange it, she gave substance to the American charge that she was inciting the tribes to war. Many Americans felt that Canada would have to be occupied before the United States would gain relief from Indian hostility. Julius W. Pratt, a scholar of this period, has argued that the whole frontier from "New Hampshire to Kentucky was insisting that the British must be expelled from Canada." This demand sprang, he has argued, from the conviction that "the British in Canada were in unholy alliance with the Western Indians, and that only by cutting off the Indians from British support could the West gain peace and security." [23] Professor Bernard Mayo has suggested that the assumption that Britain incited the Indians was generally be-

[22] *Ibid.*, XXV, 288–289.
[23] J. W. Pratt, *Expansionists of 1812* (New York, 1949), 55.

lieved and that this belief "hardened into an implacable conviction." [24] Evidence to support these views has been sought in newspapers and Congressional debates. And there is enough to give some substance to their charges. The *Lexington Reporter*, for example, stated that the only way to end Indian hostilities was to "interpose the American arm between the hands of the English and their savage allies." It concluded: "This done, the occupation of the Canadas, New Brunswick and Nova Scotia, would give us perpetual concord with the Indians . . . ." [25] The Philadelphia *Aurora* charged Britain with "letting loose of the savages with arms." [26] In Congress a similar tone characterized speeches. Felix Grundy argued that it would be of enormous value if Britain were driven from Canada so that she would "no longer have the opportunity of intriguing with our Indian neighbors and setting on the ruthless savage to tomahawk our women and children." [27]

Although these charges were made, it is unwise to give them too much weight. Even Grundy admitted that he had no proof of intrigue. "I infer," he said, that if British gold were not used, their "promise of support and a place of refuge if necessary have had their effect." [28] Others were compelled to admit that evidence to substantiate their charges was tenuous. As John Randolph said, their accusations were "destitute of any foundation beyond mere surmise and suspicion." [29] Madison himself argued in his War Message only that it was "difficult" to account for Indian warfare "without connecting" it to British influence.[30] After hostilities broke out in 1812, Clay wrote that white expansion westward, a new generation of warriors, and the propensity of savages for battle were "sufficient to account for Indian hostilities, without recurring to the most fruitful

---

[24] B. Mayo, *Henry Clay* (Boston, 1937), 307.

[25] *Lexington Reporter*, quoted Pratt, *Expansionists of 1812*, 54.

[26] Philadelphia *Aurora*, December 31, 1811, quoted Mayo, *Henry Clay*, 399.

[27] *Annals of Congress*, 12th Congress, 1st Session, I, 426.

[28] *Ibid.*, I, 425.

[29] *Ibid.*, I, 445–446.

[30] J. D. Richardson, *A Compilation of the Messages and Papers of the Presidents 1789–1897* (20 vols., Washington, 1900), I, 504.

source of them, British instigation." [31] Most knew in their hearts that unrest on the frontier did not spring from British actions. But it is easier to ascribe your troubles to villainy from abroad than to admit that it stems from your own conduct.

Just as Britain was blamed for the Indian trouble in the interior, so she was held largely responsible for the depression in the Mississippi Valley. From 1808 onward there was a steady decline in the price of Western commodities. Tobacco dropped from $8.08 per hundredweight in 1808 to $3.37 in 1811. Cotton, which sold for 22 cents a pound in 1805, sold for a mere 10 cents a pound seven years later. People affected by this catastrophe again blamed Britain for their plight. The *Lexington Reporter* observed that there were many reasons for the decline in prices but said that "the British Orders in Council which still prevent the exportation of cotton, tobacco, etc. to the Continent of Europe are the chief." [32] Undoubtedly this depression did arouse hostility toward England, but its causes were to be found in America rather than overseas. A quick boom in 1805, overexpansion, the use of marginal land—all these contributed to the economic decline in the interior. The same factors brought on worse depressions in subsequent years, but then Eastern bankers and merchants were blamed. However, in the heated atmosphere of 1811, the hand of Britain was seen everywhere.

When Congress got down to business in the autumn, the distrust and hostility felt toward Britain were reflected in the kind of men chosen to chair Congressional committees. Henry Clay, ebullient, vigorous, and determined to salvage American honor, was elected Speaker on the first ballot. It was a position that he occupied with energy and distinction. He used it to shape the tone and direction of debate, to push the policies he believed in, and to win his colleagues to his point of view. The members who composed many of the committees shared the

---

[31] Clay to Monroe, September 21, 1812, J. H. Hopkins and M. W. Hargreaves (eds.), *The Papers of Henry Clay* (Lexington, 1959), I, 729.

[32] *Lexington Reporter*, quoted G. R. Taylor, "Agrarian Discontent in the Mississippi Valley Preceding the War of 1812," *Journal of Political Economy*, vol. XXXIX, n. 4, August 1931, 500.

views of the Speaker. Clay saw to this. The crucial Foreign Affairs Committee was headed by Peter Porter of New York, and four of its eight members were War Hawks—John A. Harper, Joseph Desha, John C. Calhoun, and Felix Grundy. David R. Williams of South Carolina became chairman of the Military Affairs Committee, and a fellow Republican from his state, Langdon Cheves, headed the Naval Affairs Committee. Ezekiel Bacon of Massachusetts took over Ways and Means. All these committees had members of the opposition serving, but they had little influence. Those who had clamored for strong action held the key positions and they were not reluctant to use them. Federalists might bemoan this development, but they could no longer control the course of events.

In November Madison sent his annual message to Congress. As was customary, it reviewed the past and outlined the President's wishes for the future. It discussed Britain's position regarding the Orders in Council, nonimportation, West Florida, and the *Little Belt*. It referred to the crisis in the interior, but cautiously refrained from blaming Britain for it. It criticized France for her actions, but passed over the issue of impressment. Finally, it called for increased military preparations, but apart from vague references to the navy the President left unstated the warlike measures he felt should be taken. The message received a mixed reception. To staunch Federalists it showed Madison in his true colors—weak, confused, uncertain, and misguided. For some of his supporters it did not go far enough. The young and eager wanted a clarion call to war. Economic coercion and restraint no longer belonged in their lexicon. For too long the United States had acted patiently, and they now wanted to strike a blow for freedom. Others in the President's party were satisfied by the message. It did not go as far as they might have wished, but it clearly showed that Madison was charting a new course of action. It was up to Congress to seize the opportunity presented it and lead the country into war.

The House Committee on Foreign Relations met to consider the portions of the message that fell within its purview. The report, which it produced at the end of the month, gave a clear indication of the new mood of Congress. It briefly recounted the injuries that America had suffered at the hands of Britain and France but then went on to point out that France had rescinded her decrees. Britain, however, evinced every intention of continuing her damaging policies. The time had come, therefore, for strong measures. The United States could no longer remain indifferent to wrongs so "daring in their character, and so disgraceful in their execution." That America had not rushed into war before was due not to cowardice but rather to her love of humanity and justice. But the report added that "forbearance has ceased to be a virtue." Using the words of the President, the committee stated that it was time to put the country into the "armor and attitude" demanded by the crisis and agreeable with the nation's "spirit and expectation." [33] To this end it recommended that the military establishment be increased by 10,000 men, that the President be authorized to muster 50,000 volunteers as well as summon the militia when necessary, that the navy be put into fighting trim, and that merchant ships be armed.

The debate following the report showed the divisions of opinion that beset the country. It was quite clear that a majority of the committee contemplated war with Britain in the near future. Grundy wrote to Andrew Jackson that if "the opinion of the committee is to prevail, I may say the Rubicon is passed." [34] He continued by saying that while a majority of the committee wanted war within a given period, they also recognized that time was needed to prepare for it. In this they were supported by the administration. Monroe had met with the committee during its hearings and had told them as much. Grundy ominously concluded his letter by warning that if America did not have war or an honorable peace, people in high places would be brought down. Many Republican speakers drove home these points on the floor of the House. Opening the debate, Porter said that the committee had agreed that it was vain to expect Britain to settle her differences with America through negotiation. The question therefore was whether Ameri-

---

[33] *American State Papers, Foreign Relations*, III, 538.
[34] Grundy to Jackson, November 28, 1811, Jackson Papers, vol. IX, quoted R. Horsman, *The Causes of the War of 1812* (Philadelphia, 1963), 227.

can maritime rights should be defended by the "hazard and expense of war." [35] It was the unanimous opinion of the committee that they should. Richard Johnson of Kentucky supported this view. The tyranny of Britain, he insisted, had taken from America the "last alternatives of longer forbearance." [36] Britain had now to be opposed by war or the Declaration of Independence might just as well be formally annulled. And, he concluded, when war came the struggle should not be relinquished until Britain had renounced her system of paper blockades, her Orders in Council, and her impressment of seamen. Senator Wright of Maryland said the issue was simply one of war or submission. Impressment, he argued, was a blow at the "vitals of liberty," and Britain's interference with America's carrying trade was an injury only slightly less serious.[37] In a reasoned and calculated speech Calhoun continued the argument. The question, he said, was reduced to a single point: "Which shall we do, abandon or defend our own commercial and maritime rights, and the personal liberties of our citizens employed in exercising them? These rights are essentially attacked, and war is the only means of redress." [38]

The most articulate opponent of these views was John Randolph of Virginia. He had long fought the President's policies, and as his health deteriorated and his personality became more erratic, his distrust of the administration increased. The debate on foreign relations allowed him the opportunity to express his distaste for recent developments. In a raging speech he poured ridicule and scorn on the purveyors of war. Waves of invective rolled over the House as he assailed his opponents. This was not a war for freedom, he cried, but one for aggrandizement; it was not the preservation of freedom that the Republicans sought but the conquest of Canada. We have heard, he said, "but one word—like the whip-poor-will, but one eternal monotonous tone—Canada! Canada! Canada!" [39] Agrarian cupidity, not national honor, he charged, motivated the War Hawks.

---

[35] *Annals of Congress,* 12th Congress, 1st Session, I, 414.
[36] *Ibid.,* I, 457.
[37] *Ibid.,* I, 467.
[38] *Ibid.,* I, 478.
[39] *Ibid.,* I, 533.

Randolph's fulminations could not check the direction in which Congress was moving nor would his arguments convert his antagonists. But a realistic appraisal of all that war meant did bring caution to many. America was still a young nation with a government which, though remarkably stable, had not yet faced the shock of a major war. Although some were certain that the nation could not exist if it tolerated continued affronts to its dignity, others feared that it might not survive a military engagement with one of the world's great powers. Even if it were united in purpose, the task would be difficult; but if it were divided, as it still was, the risk would be too great.

There was a further complication, recognized by all, which came out in the debates on the committee resolutions. If war were declared, where was it to be fought? It was preposterous to think that the British Isles could be attacked. It was equally foolish to dispute Britain on the high seas. The United States did have several frigates, which could hold their own in single combat. But to pit a few frigates and a number of gunboats against the Royal Navy was like hunting elephants with peashooters. The answer to this conundrum lay at hand, however. Britain was vulnerable in Canada, and that was where the blow should be struck. As early as 1807 Gallatin had recognized this possibility and had drawn up the plans to implement it. The debates in 1811 elaborated upon this theme. Porter admitted that it would be folly to contend with Britain on the ocean, but there was a point where American power could be felt. "We could," he suggested, "deprive her of her extensive provinces lying along our border to the north." Not only were these colonies valuable in themselves, but they were also "indispensable" to Britain now that she was cut off from Europe.[40] William King, who opposed territorial expansion, insisted that Canada be taken in order to "wound our enemy in the most vulnerable part . . . ."[41] Israel Pickens urged that an attack on Canada was the only "mode in our reach for defending rights universally recognized and avowedly violated . . . ."[42] Desha

---

[40] *Ibid.*, I, 416.
[41] *Ibid.*, I, 519.
[42] *Ibid.*, I, 646.

of Kentucky, a strong supporter of war, proposed a widespread use of privateers and an "ascent" on Britain's North American possessions.[43] Lowndes of South Carolina advanced the same argument. He ridiculed Randolph's view that England could not be injured. American ships could damage British trade, and American troops could conquer Canada. Harper of New Hampshire insisted that the Canadas as well as New Brunswick, Nova Scotia, and the Bahamas should be taken. This conquest was the only way that the United States could exact payment for past damages and guard against injuries from future acts. Even the writers of a memorial from Massachusetts admitted that Canada was the only point at which Britain was assailable.

These speeches explain the real reason for the persistent references to Canada in the Twelfth Congress. It was not land hunger or Indian unrest that drove the United States to envisage the conquest of British North America. The idea that the United States would enter into a war with Britain for land that she did not need does not stand scrutiny. The theory that a coalition of frontier and Southern interests supported war so that one would take Canada while the other secured Florida is also unsubstantiated. In 1810 West Florida was occupied by America without incident. The rest of that area could be taken in the same manner. There was simply no need to declare war on Britain in order to despoil Spain. Indeed, to have done so would have been costly, devious, and senseless. And whatever we may think of Madison and the members of Congress, they were not complete fools. They were in fact deeply distressed men who were desperately anxious to find the means to combat a formidable foe. Together they struck upon the obvious and only method to wage a war. No other way was open to them; if they had not chosen this avenue of attack, they would have been criminally negligent. Only Randolph's tortuous mind could read motives of greed and expansion into their discussions. There have been wars fought for profit (and the cost of these have usually far exceeded the gain), but the War of 1812 was not one of them.

But a recognition of how the war was to be fought was only

---

[43] *Ibid.*, I, 490.

the first step. The next was to provide the means to wage the struggle. To believe that virtue was on the side of America did not mean that Providence would provide the means for victory. For that, money and men were needed in ample supply. Unfortunately, Congress did not meet this challenge. There are always those who cry that the cost of defense is too high and that heavy taxation is more dangerous to the state than an external foe. And there are always those who think that the security of the state can be achieved cheaply or that war can be waged by men armed with a clear conscience rather than a rifle. The Twelfth Congress had its fair share of these. It will be recalled that the resolutions of the Foreign Relations Committee recommended an increase in the regular army, the recruitment of volunteers, and the readying for battle of all naval vessels. There was little difficulty in securing a favorable vote for these measures. But approval in principle was one thing; implementation was quite another. The debate over the latter was sharp and revealed deep distress over the future. Senator William Giles introduced a measure calling for the creation of a regular army of 25,000 men. This figure exceeded the committee's figure by 15,000 and was intended, some have suggested, to embarrass Madison. Certainly in his speech Giles showed how inadequate a force of 10,000 would be. The British in Canada had 7,000 regulars and a sizable militia. These forces combined with the Royal Navy would enable Britain to launch attacks upon America from New York to New Orleans. To defend the nation as well as to invade Canada, he insisted, would require a larger military force than presently envisaged. While supporters of the President stood by the original request, Clay and his followers backed the new proposals, and after an extensive debate Giles's motion was approved. It is hardly necessary to add that the force was a long time in coming. Indeed, at one point Clay suggested that officers for only eight of thirteen new regiments be appointed—the remainder to be commissioned when the majority of the recruits for the original eight regiments had been enlisted. However, this precautionary action, designed in part to hold down an increase in taxes to pay for the larger army, was ultimately rejected. The new figure of 25,000 stood alone.

The debate on the militia bill was as confused as the one on the regular defense establishment. The plan was to empower the President to raise 50,000 men. But the question of where they could be used divided the House. Men like Clay and Cheves accepted the self-evident truth that soldiers should be sent where the fighting was. But others, imbued with the Republican distrust of a strong executive, opposed granting the President such powers. Because no agreement could be reached, the issue was shelved and the bill passed without reference to it. Canadians were to be grateful for Congressional views on the dangers of a strong Presidency, for on at least one important occasion state militia refused to cross into foreign soil during the heat of battle. It was a comfort to the British troops at Queenston Heights to learn that legal technicalities had prevented the reinforcement of the American army —although the latter must have had little sympathy for the strict interpreters of the Constitution who debated rather than fought.

The problem of the navy proved more difficult than that of the army. Cheves introduced a bill that would have authorized the building of twelve ships of the line and twenty frigates. Again, it seemed self-evident that in a war with Britain preparations to fight on the high seas should be made. But Republican distrust of a navy ran high. It had long been felt that a navy was a Federalist scheme designed to strengthen the executive. As Adam Seybert said, when the projected war ended the army would disband, but the navy with its train of officers would become "a powerful engine in the hands of the executive." [44] This emotional fear proved too much for the bill. Although Federalists from maritime states supported it, and Clay and Cheves argued that no war could be fought on land alone, the bill went down to defeat. Its executioners were, ironically enough, the men of the interior who voted for war.

With some measures agreed upon, Congress was next faced with the unpalatable task of providing the money to pay for them. It fell to Gallatin to draw up the administration's proposals, and they proved to be frightening. Even after modifica-

---

[44] *Ibid.*, I, 825.

tion by the Ways and Means Committee of the House, they were bad enough; they called for a doubling of import duties, a levying of direct taxes on the states, the imposition of taxes on salt and distilleries, and the introduction of a stamp tax. The prospects did not please. Some major newspapers and some Congressmen fully supported the measure. As Bacon said, "If the people will not bear the necessary taxes, it cannot be said with propriety that they will bear the contemplated war, and the sooner we know it the better." [45] But while Bacon supported the new measures, others were horrified by them and struggled to find ways of either avoiding or postponing the issue. It was argued that the taxes should not be imposed until war was declared. This argument was rather like suggesting that construction of a shelter should not begin until the tornado strikes. And yet Congress finally agreed to it. Such a decision seemed to lack martial ardor, but the House accepted the views of James Fisk who pleaded that since these were war taxes, they should not be imposed until the battle started. However, the passage of the tax bill, even in its mutilated form, was a victory for the men of war. They had secured their increases in the military establishment and had achieved the ultimate means to pay for them.

Although these steps had been taken slowly and even reluctantly, their significance should not be ignored. Even Foster, who frequently believed that Madison was blustering and bluffing, allowed doubts to creep into his mind. At the end of 1811 he wrote that he wondered whether the "United States Government are at this moment in possession of influence sufficient to prevent the two Houses from recommending an immediate declaration of war against Great Britain." Federalists, he remarked with surprise, "made no scruple of telling me that they mean to give their vote for war . . . ." [46] The last was an exaggeration, but the dangers were real enough. In December Monroe wrote, "the govt. is resolved, if G. Britain does not revoke her orders in council, in a short time, to act offensively toward her. In fact not to remain inactive and at peace, while

---

[45] *Ibid.*, I, 1102.

[46] Foster to Wellesley, No. 30, December 11, 1811, F.O. 5:77.

she wages war." [47] John Quincy Adams in Europe sensed the directions in which events were moving. "The state of our foreign relations," he said, "appear approaching to a crisis which seems to render a foreign war utterly unavoidable." [48] A month later he felt that "war with England was unavoidable." [49]

The move toward war received a further impetus from the extraordinary Henry affair. John Henry was an Irishman with all the charm of his race combined with a remarkable lack of scruples. During the *Chesapeake* crisis when many in Canada feared that war was imminent, Craig had employed him as a confidential agent. He was instructed to visit New England and report from there on the state of public opinion "both with regard to their internal politics and to the possibility of war with England," and whether in event of war Federalists "would look up to England for assistance or . . . be disposed to enter into a connexion with us." [50] When the alarm over the crisis subsided, his mission was terminated. At this point Henry sought a suitable reward for his services from the authorities in Quebec. His conception of what was fitting and Craig's were substantially different. He therefore carried his case to London where he hoped a grateful government would recognize the signal service he had rendered his country. But he was rebuffed there as well. Henry then sailed for Boston. Aboard ship he fell in with a persuasive charlatan who called himself Count Edward de Crillon. Crillon, taking advantage of Henry's burning sense of injustice, persuaded him to auction his papers to the American government. Acting as the go-between, Crillon sold them to Madison for $50,000 and then, to complete the farce, absconded with the entire sum. Henry had learned the bitter lesson that new friends were as unreliable as old employers.

The effects of the disclosure of Henry's correspondence can well be imagined. On March 9, 1812, Madison sent it to

[47] James Monroe to Joseph Monroe, December 6, 1811, Hamilton, *The Writings of James Monroe*, V, 196.
[48] Adams to Plumer, September 11, 1811, W. C. Ford (ed.), *The Writings of John Quincy Adams* (7 vols., New York, 1914), IV, 210.
[49] Adams to Eustis, October 26, 1811, *ibid.*, IV, 261.
[50] Craig to Henry, February 6, 1809, *American State Papers, Foreign Relations*, III, 546.

Congress with a special message in which he said the documents proved that in the midst of friendly negotiations the British government had sent an agent to New England to foment trouble and to intrigue with the disaffected to bring about "resistance to the laws, and eventually, in consort with a British force, of destroying the Union and forming the eastern part thereof into a political connection with Great Britain." [51] Federalists were angered and embarrassed by the documents, and newspapers took the opportunity to denounce the perfidy of England. The French minister in Washington felt that if this incident did not bring war, nothing could. Foster could not help but agree with this diagnosis. But a second look at the papers showed that they were less damaging than originally supposed. They were full of omissions and corrections. No Federalists were identified in them, and Henry would not or could not name any. The superficial qualities of the correspondence were recognized, and the episode fell into perspective. Federalists were relieved that their loyalty remained unchallenged, and Foster was grateful that the war fever whipped up by the affair was now cooling. However, the effects of the Henry affair lingered on. One of its worst results was that it convinced the British minister that the President was weak and could be bullied. As a consequence, when Foster should have been continually pressing his government to soften its attitude, he alternated his talk of the dangers of war with recommendations to stand firm.

But inflexibility by England was the one thing that would force America into action. By March 1812, war was not certain. The steps taken by Congress were not definitive, and the President still sought to avoid taking the final and irrevocable decision. His supporters were divided too, and recent news from France did not make their task easier. The difficulty that the American minister in Paris had in obtaining an audience with Napoleon was only one sign of his contempt for America. The continued ravaging of American commerce by the Emperor was another. This was so serious that there were mutterings in Congress that any declaration of war should include France. But the

---

[51] Hunt, *The Writings of James Madison*, VIII, 183.

stark impossibility of fighting a war simultaneously with two already contesting powers was self-evident. To propose it only reflected frustration. The real opponent was Britain, and the important question was whether and when the United States would reach the sticking point with her.

The patience of the War Hawks with Madison's dilatory tactics was wearing thin. On March 15 Clay saw Monroe and proposed an embargo of thirty days' duration to be followed by war if Britain had not then modified her policies. When nothing came of this, the exasperation of Clay and his followers increased. The country could not continue to live in a state of suspended animation with war probable but not certain. Finally, Monroe met with the Foreign Relations Committee and declared that the President thought that a declaration of war should be made before Congress adjourned—but only if Britain failed to abandon her course. As this appeared unlikely, war seemed a certainty. On April 1 Madison proposed a general embargo to Congress. Porter introduced a bill providing an embargo for sixty days. After short debate it was passed by a vote of 70 to 41. To Clay and Calhoun it seemed that the first step to war had been taken. The bill was then sent to the Senate where it was amended so that the embargo was to last for ninety days. Rather than prolong debate and weaken the appearance of decisiveness, the War Hawks accepted the Senate's change, and the bill became law.

It is one of the ironies of history that while America was girding herself for war, Great Britain was undergoing a major change of heart. It will be remembered that there had always been opposition to the Orders in Council and that this feeling had gathered strength and direction with the passing of time. But as long as the orders worked no serious hardships on the country, opponents of the measures were unable to influence the government. In 1811, however, England was in the depths of a serious depression, which both manufacturing and working classes blamed on these commercial decrees. What deepened the crisis in England was the news from America that Congress and the President were moving toward war. It now seemed likely that the nation that could supply the market to ease Britain's economic problem was going to join Napoleon in fighting her. The prospect of military operations in North

America with its consequent drain of men and ships caused even the Admiralty to express alarm. Because of these factors, pressure to repeal the orders became effective and powerful.

The opposition to the decrees was led by the Whigs. Baring, with his understanding of America, had long criticized the measures and he was now joined by Henry Brougham who had energy and intelligence. Brougham did not have to look far to find arguments to support his case. The depression provided them on every hand. Exports to the United States had fallen to virtually nothing. Warehouses were glutted with goods for which no overseas market could be found. The licensing system, designed to permit the movement of goods to Europe, was collapsing. Prices and wages were falling. The rate of business failures and bankruptcies was soaring. The midlands and the north were particularly hard hit. Prosperous cities like Liverpool, Leicester, Birmingham, and Sheffield were suffering massive unemployment. The cotton and woolen mills were closing their doors. The pottery works were only using two thirds of their normal work force. And so it went.

No government could ignore poverty and distress so widespread, nor could it expect the populace to bear its suffering silently. In the spring of 1812 riots broke out, and cities like Nottingham, Leeds, and Birmingham witnessed scenes of wild disorder. Troops, which would have been put to better use fighting France, were required to restore peace. The unrest in the country finally forced the government to form a committee of inquiry into the Orders in Council. The door to their repeal had been opened a crack. The committee began to hear the testimony of witnesses. Some 150 of them appeared to register their complaints. They were all businessmen, and most of them came from the center of the country. Representatives of iron, steel, textile, and pottery interests gave extensive and damning evidence. The substance of their charge was simple. There was a profound economic depression resulting almost entirely from the Orders in Council. If the decrees were repealed, the distress of the country would be remedied. One witness testified that "before the Orders in Council I had a good trade, and since them my trade is gone." [52] Although the main argument was that the

---

[52] *Minutes of Evidence Relating to the Orders in Council,* 90, quoted Horsman, *The Causes of the War of 1812,* 257.

government's policy was causing economic chaos at home, this complaint was not the only charge against the system. More sophisticated opponents of Perceval were concerned about the long-term effects of the measures. By throwing the United States on its own resources, Britain was forcing the pace of American industrialization. This acceleration would lead to a reduction of British exports in the future. Of course, the growth and diversification of America's economy could not be stopped, but they did not have to be artificially stimulated by London. For competitive reasons, then, pressure groups wanted a change in economic and foreign policy. They did not merely want Britain to cease annoying America; they wanted positive steps taken to secure American friendship. Otherwise, a good customer and a profitable market would be lost forever. The arguments of the men of business were increasingly supported by the press. There were still newspapers that backed the government, but many now called for change. The *Morning Chronicle* had long resisted the Orders in Council, but it was now joined by others. Journals like the *Edinburgh Review*, the *Gentleman's Magazine*, and *Cobbett's Political Register* denounced the government. Even *The Times*, that stately institution, began to have doubts.

But it was difficult to move the cabinet. Old and entrenched policies are always hard to change, and when a country is engaged in war, any measure justified by military necessity is valued beyond its worth. Perceval was stubborn, determined, and single-minded. These were admirable qualities in the early days of the war with France but they betrayed him now. An accommodation with America was clearly necessary, but he would not budge. A policy of firmness had worked in the past and he was convinced that it would best serve his country in the future. He was supported in this view by the familiar coalition of West Indian planters and shippers. Their arguments were old and timeworn. Again they said that the decrees were essential to Britain's war effort; again they cried that if the decrees were repealed, neutral countries would make large inroads into Britain's carrying trade.

In March the dispute came to the floor of the House of Commons; all the arguments were aired once more, and a vote taken. The government was upheld by a margin of 216 to 144. It was a defeat for the opposition, but one that gave hope to the Whigs. The Tories were being hard pressed, and it was widely believed that continued pressure would bring down the whole system. And before a month had passed, the cabinet began a cautious retreat. Castlereagh, who had replaced the lethargic Wellesley in the Foreign Office, instructed Foster to inform the United States that Britain would lift her system of licenses and limit her blockades if the Americans would renew normal trade relations. Less than two weeks later he wrote that his government would repeal the Orders in Council if France would officially renounce the Berlin and Milan Decrees. What had started as a retreat was fast turning into a rout.

A perverse fate interrupted the course of events at this critical juncture. On May 11 the Prime Minister entered the lobby of the House of Commons. He was accosted there by a demented man who harbored an illusory but fanatical grudge against him. Before a hand could be raised in defense, Perceval was shot to death. The first and only assassination of a British prime minister had taken place. For a month England was without a leader while the cabinet struggled with the task of finding a successor. Finally, agreement was reached, and Lord Liverpool took office. But during that month no action could be taken on the Orders in Council—a delay that was to prove fatal.

When the new government came into power, the situation improved rapidly. It was quite clear that the new cabinet did not want to be saddled with measures which were so intensely unpopular in the country. On June 16 Brougham, who recognized the change in mood, introduced a motion in the House of Commons to repeal the Orders in Council. One week later the cabinet gave notice that the decrees were to be withdrawn. The repeal was, however, conditional. Before it could be made permanent, the United States would have to remove its restrictions on British commerce and admit British ships of war to her ports. And even then Britain retained the right to reimpose the measures within a year if actions by the French government made it necessary. Nevertheless, a major reversal in British policy had been made.

The official reason given by Britain for this remarkable

reversal in policy was that France had finally given satisfactory notice of the renunciation of the Berlin and Milan Decrees. In May 1812, Paris published the St. Cloud Decree, dated April 28, 1811, announcing that her edicts were repealed. It was widely believed that the last date was a forgery, but this was ignored. Britain had found a face-saving device which she could use to rid herself of measures that were doing her far more harm than good. A dispatch was promptly sent to Foster instructing him to inform the American government of this new development. It arrived too late, for America had already gone to war. It has been suggested that the existence of a cable might have prevented the final rupture of relations because if Washington had known of Britain's actions, the President would not have sent his war message to Congress. This argument has a certain charm, but it is one of those hypothetical questions to which no final answer can be given. The Orders in Council constituted only one of a long list of grievances, some of which touched American honor and sovereignty more deeply and poignantly. Having worked itself up to war, Congress would hardly have backed down because one complaint had been removed. Jefferson recognized this when he wrote that the "repeal of the Orders in Council would only add recruits to our minority, and enable them the more to embarrass our march to thorough redress of our past wrongs, and permanent security for the future." [53]

While London stumbled toward a repeal of the Orders in Council, America moved toward war. The ninety-day embargo (signed into law on April 4) indicated that the moment of decision was close. On April 3, Madison wrote to Jefferson: "It appears that Perceval etc. are to retain their places, and that they prefer war with us, to a repeal of their Orders in Council. As a step to it an embargo for 60 days was recommended to Congs. on Wednesday . . . ." [54] Although Madison was privately convinced that war was nearly upon him, there was far

---

[53] Jefferson to Duane, August 14, 1812, Ford, *The Writings of Thomas Jefferson*, XI, 265.

[54] Madison to Jefferson, April 3, 1812, Hunt, *The Writings of James Madison*, VIII, 185.

less certainty in the country at large. Monroe, in a letter to the editor of the *National Intelligencer,* suggested that the embargo had not committed the administration to an irrevocable course of action. The editor himself first stated that the new move did not mean war, but less than two weeks later he reversed himself and argued that the die was now cast, and it only remained for Congress to make it official. Others were less sanguine. Federalists were divided, confused, and bitter. Some thought that the government had no choice but to push on to war. Some were convinced that the administration was still bluffing, hoping against hope that its actions would wring concessions from Britain and so save it from itself. Still others were morally certain that war would not come at all. The lack of preparedness in the country and the absence of firm direction from the President convinced them that all was not yet lost. Further, they believed that the nation was not ready to pay the price that war would exact. Military operations would be enormously costly, and worse, America would lose her valuable overseas trade. The news of the impending embargo, for example, had led to a flight of American ships laden with goods for Britain. Economic ruin stared these merchants in the face if hasty action was taken. At the very least, these men wanted time for their ships to return to the United States. Their wish for a delay was shared by those who had warehouses filled with British goods and who knew that war would put an end to their importing business. Force was given to these views by innumerable petitions calling upon the government to exercise caution and restraint.

The lack of cohesiveness in the nation was also shown in the first elections which were held before the official declaration of war in June. Supporters of war like Harper of New Hampshire were defeated, and a number of Republicans who were returned to office evinced second thoughts about fighting. Gallatin was warned about this new apathy in the nation. But more disturbing to the government than this apathy was the shift in the balance of power in two key states—Massachusetts and New York. In the spring of 1812 Federalists captured both the governorship and the legislature of Massachusetts. One of the first acts of the state's new government was passage of a resolution denouncing the prospects of war. Events in New York were equally critical for the administration, but the issues were more complicated. Here was a state that was largely Republican in nature and that gradually and firmly assumed a posture of opposition toward the President. This development came about because of a splintering of the Republican party in New York. A group led by George and De Witt Clinton split off from Madison and pitted its strength against him. It has generally been assumed that political ambition and a desire for power motivated this action. William Crawford of Georgia wrote, "They were a set of Malcontents, who are more intent upon making De Witt Clinton President, than they are desirous of promoting the public good." [55] But the picture was more complicated than this. Indeed, complications bedeviled motives in 1812, for men were torn by differences of opinion on how best to protect American interests. What does seem clear is that the Clintonians had become deeply suspicious of both the ability and the intentions of the President. They had viewed with alarm Jefferson's embargo, for they were convinced that this kind of commercial policy would serve their country badly and ultimately destroy their party. Commercial interests in New York could not survive the kind of economic retaliation that Jefferson and then Madison employed; they preferred a policy of negotiation based upon military and naval strength. Therefore they were prepared for and voted for increased military appropriations. But by 1812 they were convinced that they were not getting the strength they sought. Instead they believed they were receiving erratic leadership from a President who could no longer be trusted. He seemed to be favoring policies that cultivated support in the South and the West and that could spell disaster for his party in the North and East. They saw the rising strength of Federalism in the North and East as a popular reaction to a weak President, and they were determined not to go down with him.

Their breaking point came with Madison's recommendation of a sixty-day embargo. This clearly seemed to them the first

---

[55] Crawford to Milledge, Crawford Ms., LC, quoted R. Brown, *The Republic in Peril 1812* (New York, 1964), 141.

step to war. And although it would be a war with the right enemy and fought in the right place, they were emphatic in their view that the time was wrong. They knew how ill-prepared the country was, and they realized how exposed to attack were their ports and northern borders. They had voted to strengthen the military establishmen ... the nation, but the President had not moved rapidly enough to implement their recommendations. They wanted, therefore, to postpone a final break with Britain. A Senator from New York said he had been prepared to vote for war in November but was not in June. None of them believed in war first and preparation second. The President had, in their view, reversed his order of priorities. The other arguments about the cost of war, the dangers to the economy, and the loss of overseas markets were also used. But these arguments were less significant than the conviction that monumental mismanagement in Washington was fast placing the government, the nation, and the Republican party in danger of oblivion. It is possible, of course, that all these views were merely cover for self-seeking politicians who saw in an international crisis the opportunity to advance their own careers. The state in danger is a cry that has frequently been raised by the unscrupulous and the ambitious. But the views of the Clintonians were shared by many honorable and troubled men.

Although some elements of the nation seemed cursed with uncertainty and the forces opposed to Madison appeared to be gathering strength, the War Hawks continued to drive relentlessly and successfully toward war. Toward the end of March, Calhoun wrote:

I think on the whole things go well here. Congress has passed all necessary legislation for a vigorous campaign. It now rests with the Executive. Their Zeal and intelligence cannot now be doubted. At the commencement of the session I felt much alarm, as I thought I saw in some of the members of the cabnit [sic] a disinclination to the measures adopted and an apparent want of Zeal in most of them. The case is now very different.[56]

Clay wrote after the embargo that it was a measure "not

---

[56] Calhoun to Noble, March 22, 1812, R. L. Meriwether (ed.), *The Papers of John C. Calhoun* (Columbia, South Carolina, 1959), I, 95.

designed as the substitute of War, but as a component part of the system which government is deliberately forming." [57] Calhoun agreed. He called the embargo "a decisive step" that "is understood to be a prelude to war." He only felt concern over the lack of leadership from Madison. "Our President," he wrote, "tho a man of amiable manners and great talents, has not I fear those commanding talents, which are necessary to controul [sic] those about him. He permits devisions [sic] in his cabinet. He reluctantly gives up the system of peace." [58]

But he did give it up. During April Congress argued and discussed but did not legislate. In the middle of the month it very nearly voted itself a recess until the second week of May. This recess was beaten down by the War Hawks, for a Congress dispersed would be one unable to act. The inaction of Congress during these weeks was not solely the result of a confusion of spirit or uncertainty among its members. Rather, all Washington was waiting for the arrival of the *Hornet* from Europe with dispatches from Paris and London. If the news from Britain was unfavorable, the President would go on to war. But if it held a promise of relief, the government was ready to reconsider its policies. On May 22 the *Hornet* docked. She bore reports from France that disheartened America, for Napoleon had given no evidence of a change of heart. Reports from England were quite as bad. The American chargé d'affaires there reported that the Orders in Council were under attack but held out no hope for their repeal. Castlereagh's instructions to Foster were as discouraging. The Foreign Secretary affirmed that France had not repealed her decrees and that the only concession that Britain was prepared to offer was a modification or perhaps abolition of the licensing system. Although this would have opened Europe to American trade, it was too trifling a concession to be taken seriously.

At the end of the month Foster discussed with the administration the latest British offer. His was a hopeless task. To

[57] Clay to Worsely, April 4, 1812, Hopkins and Hargreaves, *The Papers of Henry Clay*, I, 643.

[58] Calhoun to Macbride, April 18, 1812, Meriwether, *The Papers of John C. Calhoun*, I, 99–100.

insist that the United States reverse herself over the alleged repeal of the Berlin and Milan Decrees was futile. To state that Britain would not surrender her maritime practices was to invite disaster. The failure of Britain to make meaningful concessions in the spring of 1812 made war a certainty. The British minister's meetings with Madison and Monroe took place on May 27 and 28. On June 1 the President sent his war message to Congress. Foster had clung for months to the illusion that war could and would be avoided. Even during the ninety-day embargo he had remained hopeful. But by May he began to feel that both countries were on a collision course. On May 4 he wrote that "as far as I am able to judge from the language of both Gentlemen [Madison and Monroe] it seems to me that it is really decided by the American Government that they will not recede from the line of conduct that they have adopted, but endeavor preferably to produce a war between the two Countries." [59] Ten days later Foster said that the government was diligently "spreading intimations of their having come to a final decision to declare war against England if the majority will support them." [60] Finally, he sent the grim message in June that, all efforts at reconciliation having failed, the President had sent his war message to Congress.

First in that document's list of grievances was impressment— a practice that Madison called a "crying enormity" against which the "United States have in vain exhausted remonstrances and expostulations." The President next charged: "British cruisers have been in the practice also of violating the rights and the peace of our coasts. They hover over and harass our entering and departing commerce." The third complaint concerned "pretended blockades" under the guise of which American "commerce has been plundered in every sea . . . ." The fourth dealt with "the sweeping system of blockades, under the name of the Orders in Council . . . ." Finally, the President insinuated that there was a relationship between the British in Canada and the Indian unrest on the frontier.[61] The charges of Madison

---

[59] Foster to Castlereagh, No. 34, May 5, 1812, F.O. 5:85.

[60] Foster to Castlereagh, No. 35, May 15, 1812, F.O. 5:85.

[61] Richardson, *Messages and Papers of the Presidents*, 1, 499–505.

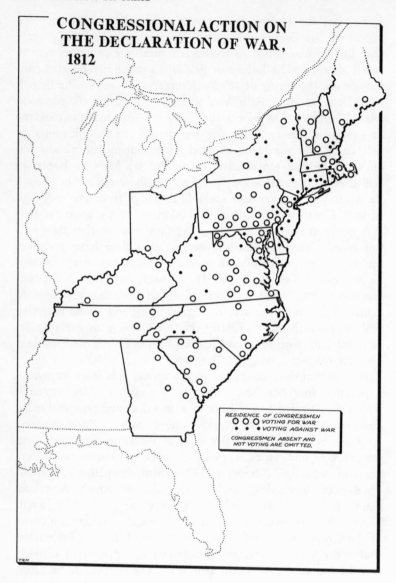

CONGRESSIONAL ACTION ON
THE DECLARATION OF WAR,
1812

RESIDENCE OF CONGRESSMEN
○ ○ ○ VOTING FOR WAR
• • • VOTING AGAINST WAR
CONGRESSMEN ABSENT AND
NOT VOTING ARE OMITTED.

were delivered in the order of their gravity. The first was impressment and this was only right and proper. That little had been heard of it in the past two years did not mean that America had forgotten or forgiven this practice. It simply reflected the sure knowledge that negotiating on this subject was a waste of time. Britain had no intention of giving up the impressment that she deemed essential to her security. Nearly a generation later when a motion to abolish the practice was introduced into the House of Commons, hardly a member voted in its favor. Palmerston said at the time that public opinion supported impressment and that no government could risk the censure that would fall upon its head if it were abandoned. What still had so much support in the 1830s was even more intensively supported at the height of the Napoleonic Wars. But nothing struck harder at the roots of American sovereignty or challenged more seriously her ability to protect her citizens. The other reasons for war—blockades and the Orders in Council—were dealt with carefully and fully. Madison did not need to do this because all Americans knew how much they were damaging their country. But the President wished to make his case strong and impervious. When the message was concluded, Congress went into secret session for debate. Two weeks passed before the declaration of war was approved. The House acted with speed, voting on the measure on June 4, but Senate approval was not secured until June 17. One day later Foster was summoned to the State Department where he was told that a state of war existed between Britain and America.

The nature of the vote on the declaration of war and the margin by which it was passed have long been sources of contention. The vote in the House of Representatives was 79 to 49, while the vote in the Senate was 19 to 13. America has never entered a foreign war so deeply divided. Nations are often divided over the necessity of fighting, but at the moment of decision there is usually a closing of ranks. But this did not happen in 1812. Most of those who were adamantly opposed to war refused to be moved by cries for unity or appeals to patriotism. They cast their votes against the declaration and, having entered the struggle reluctantly, they supported it grudgingly. Because of this division it is particularly important to understand the forces that were at work in this reluctant Congress.

It has been frequently argued that the support for war was sectional, and that it was brought on by a coalition of frontiersmen and Southerners whose motives included pride and self-interest. These men, it has been suggested, wanted to preserve American honor by fighting. But at the same time they expected by taking Canada and Florida to gain territory to satisfy their expansionist dreams. Although the crescent of western states from Ohio to Tennessee supported war, these two states and Kentucky had only nine votes. All of them were cast for war, but they did not provide the support that was necessary for success. Indeed, even if they had been withheld or thrown against the President, war would still have come. There also were frontiersmen in Pennsylvania and New York, of course, but no proof exists that they voted for sectional reasons. The bulk of the support for war came from the Middle and Southern states. Pennsylvania (16), Virginia (14), Maryland (6), North Carolina (6), and South Carolina (8), provided fifty of the votes favoring the declaration. The rest (save for the western ones referred to) came from the Northeast. The seventeen votes from this area (Massachusetts giving six) were vitally important, for if they had been mustered against Madison, he would have failed. All these areas were deeply affected by Britain's policies on the high seas. From Portsmouth, New Hampshire, down through Philadelphia and Baltimore to Savannah, Georgia, there was registered an enormous tonnage of shipping. The effects of impressment and the Orders in Council were severely felt on the Atlantic seaboard, and it is hardly surprising that so many of its Congressmen joined with the administration in calling for war. An exception to this pattern—and it was a notable one—was New York. Here was a state very much like Pennsylvania in that it had manufacturing, commercial, and maritime interests as well as a western frontier. Yet it voted eleven to three against war. The hostility of the Clintonians to the President, however, goes far to explain the conduct of New York politicians. Their opposition was rooted in the belief that Madison was a weakling and would be unable to provide the leadership that would be necessary in such a contest.

It has also been suggested that the vote in the House of Representatives reflected sectional interests less than it did party division. Most Federalists voted against war while some 90 per cent of the Republicans supported the administration. Although a few, like Randolph who had forsaken the party in spirit if not in name, opposed war, the bulk of the Republicans rallied to the President. To have done otherwise would have meant a political betrayal of Madison of such a monumental nature that it might well have destroyed the party. Thus the majority of those Republicans who had reservations about the timing of the war buried them and supported the President in June. But it would be unwise to think that it was simply party regularity that led men to support Madison. Most Republicans, whether young or old, simply felt that the time for haggling, negotiating, and debating had passed and that national honor required that the enemy be engaged.

The Senate acted more slowly than the House, and the vote was even closer. A solid core of Senators were strongly opposed to war with Britain. There were, in addition, some Republicans who appeared, for a variety of reasons, to be ready to swing against the administration. When the committee reported the bill for war to the floor, the fight was joined. On June 10 Senator Gregg introduced a resolution that would have substituted naval reprisals for war. And it passed by 17 votes to 13. It is difficult to imagine what the sponsors of this measure hoped to gain by it. Had it been accepted by the government, it would have delayed the outbreak of war on the land, but it would also have led to conflict on the high seas. Surely no one could have seriously believed it possible to confine the war to water. Two days later a further resolution was introduced designed to mete out equal treatment to France and Britain. But this even more extraordinary action was defeated. A triangular war was more absurd than a limited one with Britain on the ocean. Then Senator Gregg's original motion was brought to the floor again, but this time it was defeated. It was becoming clear that a partial war with Britain was impossible. The choice seemed to lay between submission to her practices or military defiance. A majority finally chose military defiance. On June 17 the doubters fell into line, and the declaration of war passed by six votes. It was, as the Duke of Wellington said of Waterloo, "a damned serious business . . . the nearest thing you ever saw in your life." The President and those who wanted strong action had finally pulled the nation into a conflict that most wanted to avoid but that a majority recognized could no longer be postponed.

This was not a war entered upon with national fervor or romantic enthusiasm. There were, of course, some who felt that the battles would be short and victory swift. Canada, with its large American population, would fall to the famous Kentucky militia in a week. Jefferson wrote that "the acquisition of Canada this year, as far as the neighborhood of Quebec, will be a mere matter of marching . . . ." [62] Events were to prove how foolish such a conception was. The war would be long and bloody—and many of the engagements fierce and closely fought. Those who envisaged an arduous and prolonged adventure were right—they almost always are. But apart from a few enthusiasts, America entered the conflict in a troubled state of mind. And for a century and a half various theories have been offered in explanation of this reluctance.

In 1939 there was a clear consensus in Britain that Hitler should be opposed, and in that fateful September when Poland was invaded, hardly a voice was raised against a declaration of war. In December 1941, the attack on Pearl Harbor gave the United States no choice but to defend herself at once and with all her energy. These were clear-cut instances in which national agreements existed and governments would have been brought down had they not acted as they did. But if there was a consensus in 1812, it was not unanimous. And such as it was, it had been a long time in coming. Henry Adams said that the grounds for war, though strong in 1812, were weaker than they had been in June 1808 or January 1809. Why, then, did the declaration come when it did? The answers to this question have been

---

[62] Jefferson to Duane, August 4, 1812, P. L. Ford (ed.), *The Writings of Thomas Jefferson* (10 vols., New York, 1892–1899), XII, 265.

diverse and even contradictory. Historians Alfred T. Mahan, Henry Adams, and A. L. Burt have emphasized the conflict over maritime rights. They have suggested that the disputes over impressment, the Orders in Council, and to a lesser extent paper blockades, contraband, and the Rule of 1756 were so insoluble that war was bound to come. Others, such as Louis Hacker and Pratt, were concerned with what appeared to be the highly sectional nature of the vote and sought their answers in land hunger or anger over Indian depredations committed on frontier settlements. Taylor saw regional forces at work, too, but argued that it was economic distress in the South and West, brought on by the Orders in Council, that drove these areas to war. More recently, Reginald Horsman and Bradford Perkins have stressed the complicated nature of the war's origins. The European wars created problems for America that were unexpected and difficult of solution. More perceptive diplomacy might have saved the situation, but, as Perkins suggests, Madison and Jefferson never rose to the heights that the crisis demanded.

The divided views on the causes of the war reflect, in part, the confusion existing in the country itself in 1812. But perhaps too much attention has been focused upon regional, sectional, and economic differences. The challenge to America was shared by all her citizens; the major differences arose over the means and methods for dealing with them. There can be no doubt that America's problems sprang from Europe's wars. In 1794 Jay's Treaty settled a number of grave Anglo-American differences. But it did not resolve the maritime disputes that were becoming increasingly serious. These were temporarily shelved when peace came in 1801, but they burst forth with greater force with the renewal of the struggle in 1803. From then until 1812 the United States was faced with practices which directly challenged her honor and her position. British impressment on the high seas affected Americans directly and emotionally. The insistence by London that Britain had the right to the services of all British subjects and the duty to secure these, even if it meant searching American ships in international waters, was bound to be dangerous. If impressment were deemed absolutely necessary to Britain's survival—and rightly or wrongly it was—

then it was also properly considered to be a challenge to American sovereignty. If the flag of the United States could not protect her citizens, of what use was it? The Revolution had been fought for independence, and now independence was being threatened again.

What was true of impressment was also true of the Orders in Council. The government in London considered these decrees to be absolutely essential to the fight against Napoleon. Admittedly they also served British commercial interests in their struggle with American competitors and this consideration was taken into account when they were drafted. The United States could not help but see them as damaging to her economy and to her freedom. The general rights of neutrals to trade freely during wartime were widely recognized in the late eighteenth and early nineteenth centuries, and the new British doctrines of blockade and economic control were an affront to America. The enforcement of the Rule of 1756, the disputes over "free ships, free goods" and over broken and continuous voyages simply added to the simmering discontent in Washington. When an economic depression wasted large portions of the country and when Indian unrest threatened its borders, the simmering discontent boiled over into demands for war. The actions of France, too, harmed America. But France did not control the high seas as did Britain nor was she vulnerable to pressure through Canada, as was England. Further, though Napoleon might seize American ships, he frequently did it under the guise of municipal regulations. These facts were well understood by Jefferson who wrote that "France has kept pace with England in iniquity of principle, although not in the power of inflicting wrongs on us." [63] If the roles of Britain and France had been reversed, who can doubt that America would have gone to war with Napoleon.

The challenge faced by Jefferson and Madison was the most serious since the winning of independence. Madison had no illusions about the extent or gravity of the situation. Soon after the war started he wrote:

---

[63] Jefferson to Kosciusko, June 28, 1812, *ibid.*, XI, 259.

When the U.S. assumed & established their rank among the Nations of the Earth, they assumed & established a common Sovereignty on the high seas, as well as an exclusive sovereignty within their territorial limits. The one is as essential as the other to their Character as an Independent Nation. However conceding they may have been on controvertible points, or forbearing under casual and limited injuries, they can never submit to wrongs irreparable in their kind, enormous in their amount, and indefinite in their duration; and which are avowed and justified on principles degrading the U. States from the rank of a sovereign and independent Power.[64]

This was the heart of the matter. The sovereignty of the state itself was at stake. And when this was recognized, regional and sectional interests paled into insignificance. The challenge was to every American, and the preservation of the nation required that all muster to the flag. Recognition of the problem did not mean that its solution would be easy. Britain was fighting for her life and was not much concerned with legal niceties and international fictions. She would use force when it suited her purpose. Gradually Americans understood that this force would have to be answered by force. The United States was slow in coming to this understanding not because Jefferson was pacific in nature or because Madison could not screw up his courage to the testing point. Rather it was because Britain was one of the great world powers, and prudence and good sense demanded that peaceful negotiations be exhausted before other measures were considered. In the years from 1803 to 1812 the United States made one attempt after another to secure relief from British and French practices. Every means, short of war, was tried—endless discussion, entreaties, and economic coercion. They all failed. Either American views were not successfully portrayed, or Britain did not care deeply enough about the United States. It was, of course, the latter. London would have preferred American friendship, but she would not buy it if the price was surrender of her maritime practices.

So it was that after nine years of futile bargaining the United

---

[64] Madison to ...., July 25, 1812, Hunt, *The Writings of James Madison*, VIII, 205.

States finally decided that war was better than submission. Unfortunately there were those in the country who felt that negotiations were still feasible or that the wrong enemy had been chosen or that the cost of battle would be too high. Some in Massachusetts said that the conquest of Canada "would afford no indemnification, if achieved, for the losses to which we should be exposed upon our unprotected seaboard and upon the ocean." [65] Others, largely Federalist in allegiance, believed that Britain was the last hope of ordered and good government and that to attack her would betray these principles. They suggested that American diplomacy had failed in its duty and that Britain was not fully aware of the depth of American feeling on certain subjects. Perhaps they were right, but it is doubtful that better men could have secured more advantageous terms. London was in no mood to compromise as long as France was the enemy.

In any event, by June 1812, a majority in Congress had decided that America would have to fight in order to survive. How could a government hold up its head if it could not protect its citizens? How could the Republic itself (let alone the Republican party) continue to exist if it did not rise to the challenge? When Calhoun talked of a second war of independence, he was not far from the mark. A young country was on trial. Its test would be whether it could survive in the harsh world of reality. That it did so under the leadership of a President who lacked both the imagination and the capacity to fire the enthusiasm of his countrymen said much for its intrinsic strength.

---

[65] *Annals of Congress*, 12th Congress, 1st Session, I, 260.

CHAPTER V

A Lasting Peace

THE DECLARATION OF WAR in 1812 marked the decision by the President and Congress that force alone would uphold their nation's interest and honor. And having decided on this militant course of action, they should have let nothing deflect them from it. But instead of vigorously prosecuting the war, the President entertained advances for a truce from Britain—and peace.

The first attempt to stop the fighting before it began came from the British minister in Washington the day after the declaration of war. Foster suggested to Monroe that hostilities might be suspended until the formal notice of the declaration was received in London. During that period, he said, he could take to England any proposals that the United States might wish to make. This suggestion was rejected, and diplomatic relations between the two countries were officially severed. But four days later when Foster was taking leave of the President, he asked whether a repeal of the Orders in Council could lead to a restoration of peace. Madison replied that a repeal, if accompanied by a pledge to negotiate on impressment, might be helpful. Thinking that the President was opening the door to peace, Foster then urged that hostilities be suspended until further news was received from England. But Madison refused to entertain the notion. He could do nothing else. In the first place, Congressional reaction to such a move would have been violent. One can well imagine the anger with which Calhoun and Clay would have greeted a step that they could only deem to be retrogressive and cowardly. In the second place, agreement to this proposal would have made it difficult for Madison again to whip up the nation's enthusiasm for fighting. Martial ardor is not a commodity to be turned on and off like water. And finally, of course, the President rejected the offer because he could not bring himself to believe that a temporary truce would lead Britain to make any meaningful concessions. He thought that Britain was utterly and inflexibly committed to the Orders in Council. By the logic of history he should have been right, but he was wrong; on the very day of Foster's meeting with him, Britain repealed the measures in question. When the President finally learned of this astonishing reversal of policy, he was taken aback, but he attributed the cabinet's actions to a combination of American firmness and internal British pressures. "I think it not improbable," he wrote, "that the sudden change in relation to the Orders in Council, first in yielding to a qualified suspension, and then a repeal, was the effect of apprehensions in the Cabinet that the deliberation of Congs. would have upon that issue, and that the Ministry could not stand agst. the popular torent agst. the Orders in Council, swelled as it would be by the addition of a war with the U.S. . . . ." [1] But at the time of Foster's approach he had no inkling of the shifts that were taking place in British policy, and so he acted as he did.

Yet the administration reversed itself only one week after this expression of determined forcefulness, for Monroe wrote to Jonathan Russell, the American chargé in London, suggesting that he discuss the possibility of arranging a truce with the government there. This truce could be accomplished, he said, if the Orders in Council were repealed, if no illegal blockades were substituted for them, and if orders were given to cease impressment as well as to return those seamen already forcibly taken from American vessels. As an inducement to Britain to accept these terms, Monroe instructed Russell to assure Britain that Congress would pass a law barring British seamen from serving aboard either the public or commercial vessels of the United States. Russell was also instructed to inform London that his government would not press immediately for compensation for damages suffered under the Orders in Council, al-

---

[1] Madison to Jefferson, August 17, 1812, Gaillard Hunt (ed.), *The Writings of James Madison* (7 vols., New York, 1900–1910), VIII, 212.

though such claims were ultimately to be made in any final peace settlement.

It seems difficult to believe that one week of warfare without bloodshed had convinced Monroe that peace was an imperative. It is quite as difficult to believe that he honestly expected to exact such extravagant terms from Britain without fighting, for he was asking her to surrender all those practices upon which her naval supremacy presumably rested. Yet some consideration had moved the Secretary of State to take this extraordinary step. It was, simply, that Monroe had concluded that a lengthy war would lead to a complication rather than a resolution of Anglo-American differences. He said to Russell:

> . . . it will . . . occur that a prosecution of the War for one year, or even a few months, if not for a shorter term, will present very serious obstacles on the part of the United States to an accommodation, which do not now exist. I will advert to one only. Should our troops enter Canada you will perceive the effect which that measure cannot fail to have, by the compromitment [sic] it might make of the United States, to the inhabitants of the British Provinces and the effect which success (which could not fail to attend it) might have on the public mind here, making it difficult to relinquish Territory which had been conquered.[2]

But when Russell, acting on these instructions, informed Castlereagh that a new revocation of the Orders in Council was required because of the American declaration of war, he was briskly told that such a request was wholly unacceptable. And when Russell told the Foreign Secretary that the cessation of impressment was required by the United States, he was frankly and firmly informed that Britain would never "consent to suspend the exercise of a right upon which the naval strength of the empire mainly depends . . . ." Castlereagh later told Russell bluntly that not only did Russell fail to appreciate the "great sensibility and jealousy of the people of England on this subject" but also that "no administration could expect to remain in power that should consent to renounce the right of impressment, or to suspend the practice, without the certainty of an

---

[2] Monroe to Russell, June 26, 1812, S. M. Hamilton (ed.), *The Writings of James Monroe* (7 vols., New York, 1898–1903), V, 212–213.

arrangement which should obviously be calculated most un-equivocally to secure its objects." [3]

This rejection of terms ended Russell's efforts to secure a truce, for it was apparent that Britain would not pay the price America was asking. Nor could the United States reduce her terms. She had gone to war to put an end to certain British practices, and she could not in conscience stop before she had secured relief from the most odious of them. Indeed, some argued that her demands should be higher than before. Jefferson said:

The British government seem to be doing later what done earlier might have prevented war; to wit: repealing the orders in council. But it should take more to make peace than to prevent war. The sword once drawn, full justice must be done. "Indemnification for the past and security for the Future," should be painted on our banners.[4]

Jefferson's views were shared by the administration. It may seem that the Treaty of Ghent reversed this position by ignoring impressment. But when it was signed in 1814, the defeat of Napoleon had automatically put an end to the very practice that had prevented the truce in 1812.

Russell's failure in London was paralleled by the failure of British efforts in America to stop hostilities. In the United States two separate attempts were made to end the fighting. It will be recalled that Foster, after pleading unsuccessfully with Madison to suspend hostilities until news had come from England, took formal leave of the President. The British minister traveled to Halifax where he was to board a ship for England. He had been there only a short time when he received a dispatch from Castlereagh informing him of Britain's intention to repeal the Orders in Council. He promptly instructed Baker, the British chargé d'affaires in Washington, to communicate the news to the American government. Because Monroe was in Virginia, Baker was forced to deal with John Graham, the

---

[3] Castlereagh to Russell, August 29, 1812, *American State Papers, Foreign Relations*, III, 589.

[4] Jefferson to Wright, August 8, 1812, A. A. Lipscomb and A. E. Bergh (eds.), *The Writings of Thomas Jefferson* (20 vols., Library Edition, Washington, 1903), XIII, 184.

chief clerk in the State Department. Graham hastily transmitted the information to Madison who received it with "sincere satisfaction as opening a door to an early and satisfactory termination of existing hostilities. . . ." [5] The President also said that he would welcome more specific information and observed that in any case Russell had full powers to arrange a truce. On August 12 the information that Madison wanted arrived in Washington. It was a copy of the repeal of the Orders in Council. Baker immediately suggested to Monroe that a truce be agreed upon but was told that nothing could be done until the cabinet had received news of Russell's work in London.

While Baker was busy in Washington, Foster was doing his best in Halifax to arrange a military truce in the Northeast. He instructed Sir George Prevost, the Governor-in-Chief of Canada, to send a message to General Dearborn, in command of the American forces in the East, suggesting the desirability of suspending any action by troops under him. The message added that, while General Hull's forces would have to be driven from Canada, it was hoped that Dearborn would give "such orders to the troops employed on that service, as shall prevent any further movement . . . ." [6] General Dearborn agreed to a temporary truce while he waited for instructions from Washington. At the end of the month he received a note from Madison ordering him to reject a truce and to launch an immediate attack upon Canada. These instructions decisively ended any hopes for an early peace. Once the fighting had spread from the Great Lakes to the Atlantic Ocean, it would be a long time before it could be stopped.

This course of action, Madison felt, was the only one that would protect the maritime and military interests of the United States. Because the "principal object of the war," he said, "is to obtain redress against the British practice of impressment, an agreement to suspend hostilities, even before the British government is heard from on that subject, might be considered a relinquishment of that claim." Further, he stated, his administration could not admit the right of Britain to "restore the

---

[5] Baker to Castlereagh, #19, August 10, 1812, F.O. 5:87.
[6] Prevost to Dearborn, August 2, 1812, F.O. 5:87.

orders in council . . . under circumstances of which she alone is the judge . . . ." If there were sound reasons involving maritime rights for rebuffing Britain, there were equally valid military ones for spurning her. The President observed that "no security is given or proposed as to the Indians," and since "they can only be restrained by force when once let loose," the American army must be free to act. But far more important than its failure to restrain the Indians was the fact that the truce "restrains the United States from acting where their power is greatest, and leaves Great Britain at liberty and gives her time to augment her forces in our neighborhood."[7] Madison reverted to this theme in a subsequent letter to Jefferson in which he wrote:

As we do not apprehend invasion by land, and preparations on each side were to be restrained, nothing could be gained by us, whilst arrangements & reinforcements adverse to Hull might be decisive; and on every supposition the Indians wd. continue to be active agst. our frontiers, the more so in consequence of the fall of Michilimackinac. Nothing but triumphant operations on the Theatre which forms their connection with the Enemy will control their bloody inroads.[8]

Madison placed his finger squarely on the key to victory when he observed that time best served England. If the United States could strike immediately and forcefully into the heart of Canada, she might well control that country before reinforcements could arrive from across the ocean.

The collapse of the truce in the Northeast was shortly followed by the failure of the final British effort to secure an early end to the war. On September 30, Admiral Warren, the British commander of naval forces in the Western Hemisphere wrote to Monroe that his government had authorized him to propose "the immediate cessation of hostilities between the two countries . . . ."[9] Monroe replied that while Washington would

---

[7] Secretary of State to Russell, August 21, 1812, *American State Papers, Foreign Relations*, III, 588.

[8] Madison to Jefferson, August 17, 1812, Hunt, *The Writings of James Madison*, VIII, 213.

[9] Warren to the Secretary of State, September 30, 1812, *Report on Canadian Archives*, 1896, 71, n. B.

welcome any opportunity to terminate the war, no peace would be lasting that did not settle the problem of impressment. He reiterated his government's willingness to prohibit the employment of British subjects on American ships but insisted that this prohibition must be matched by a British pledge to stop the practice which had so injured America. Warren, of course, could do no more. Castlereagh had made it clear that Britain would not compromise on this issue. A continuation of the war under these circumstances was inevitable.

It has been suggested that during these extraordinary exchanges of notes Madison shifted the grounds for making war from the Orders in Council to impressment. But this was hardly the case. The President had always made it abundantly clear that there were two paramount principles at stake: America's right to trade freely in the world and her obligation to protect her seamen from unlawful seizure. When Britain repealed her Orders in Council, only one half of America's minimum demands had been met. Before Madison called a halt to the fighting, the other half would have to be settled.

During the negotiations between Russell and Castlereagh in the autumn of 1812, Russell had promised that America would pass a law prohibiting the employment of British seamen in the public or private vessels of the United States. This offer had been made in the hopes that it would induce Britain to discontinue impressment, and even though the Foreign Secretary had insisted then that Britain would never give up a practice so vital to her security, the United States enacted the promised legislation. In March 1813, Madison signed into law an act which stated that the United States would exclude foreign seamen from her shipping after the war. In enacting this legislation Congress and the President were depriving their country of the services of thousands of seamen without securing any concessions in return. It was an act of self-sacrifice without justification and can only be explained on the grounds that Madison was so desperate to secure a cessation of impressment that he was prepared to take any and every action to that end.

The enactment of this particular legislation coincided with a Russian offer to mediate a peace between Britain and America.

The Tsar wanted to secure an Anglo-American accord because Russia was deeply disturbed by the loss of her trade with America and even more concerned over the prospective divergence of British troops from the peninsula to Canada. If this happened there would be increased French pressure upon her. Tsar Alexander decided, therefore, to offer his services as a mediator. As early as September 1812, the idea of mediation had been broached to John Quincy Adams, American minister to Russia. Count Romanzoff had said that the Tsar felt an amicable agreement between America and Britain might be arranged more easily by discreet negotiations than by direct talks. He asked Adams whether he knew of any objections his government might have to the Tsar's offering his services as a mediator. Adams replied that he could not speak authoritatively on the matter but was not aware "of any obstacle or difficulty which would occasion" his government to "decline accepting it." [10]

After receiving this assurance, the Russian government sent instructions to Daschkoff, the Russian minister in Washington, to offer the services of the Tsar as mediator. He made the offer in March 1813. Three days after receiving Daschkoff's note, Monroe replied that the President "willingly accepts the mediation of your sovereign to promote peace between the United States and Great Britain." [11] Madison's eagerness to take up the Russian offer was largely due to the turn that events had taken. The invasion of Canada had fallen terribly short of the President's expectations. Everything that the United States had put her hand to had failed. America's troubles were the result of incompetent planning and faulty execution. When war was declared American forces should have struck quickly at Montreal, for control of that city would have made possible control of all of Canada above it. But the expectation of support from the American population in Upper Canada prompted the United States to launch her forces at the Niagara region. However, the settlers of Upper Canada did not flock to the American

---

[10] C. F. Adams (ed.), *John Quincy Adams, Memoirs* (12 vols., Philadelphia, 1874–1877), II, 402.

[11] Secretary of State to Daschkoff, March 11, 1813, *American State Papers, Foreign Relations*, III, 624.

banner, and the British forces there were ably led. General
Hull surrendered at Detroit in August 1812; when the American army crossed at Niagara that October, it was thrown back
at Queenston Heights by forces under General Brock. Upper
Canada had been saved for Britain. The picture was little better
elsewhere from the American point of view. Quebec and Montreal remained untouched, and the Maritimes stood in splendid
isolation. On the ocean American privateers harmed British
shipping, but their actions proved to be irritating rather than
fatal. The Royal Navy controlled the high seas, and as long
as America had no substantial fleet she would suffer the consequences. No one in the United States had expected that fighting the war would prove so difficult or that the enemy forces
in Canada would be so stubborn in battle. Toward the end of
1813 America's position improved, but the events of 1812 were
somber and disheartening. Quite as serious as the military reverses was the domestic crisis facing the President. The war had
not united the nation, as so many had hoped and expected.
Instead of arousing a crusading spirit, it had only deepened
and hardened feelings of bitterness. Both New York and New
England were forceful opponents of the struggle, and their entrenched hostility to the President's policies threatened the unity
of the nation. Given these circumstances, it is little wonder that
Madison was willing to accept the mediation of Russia.

But he would not have favored the Tsar's intervention if
he had not believed that America's maritime rights would be
protected in the discussions. Because Russia's views on this
subject closely paralleled Washington's, he was prepared to
open negotiations. He said at the time:

We are encouraged in this policy by the known friendship of the
Emperor Alexander to this country; and by the probability that the
greater affinity between the Baltic and American idea of maritime
law, than between those of the former and of G.B. will render his
interposition as favorable as will be consistent with the character
assumed by him.[12]

Having accepted Tsar Alexander's good offices, Madison was

---

[12] Madison to Nicholas, April 12, 1813, Hunt, *The Writings of James Madison*, VIII, 243–244.

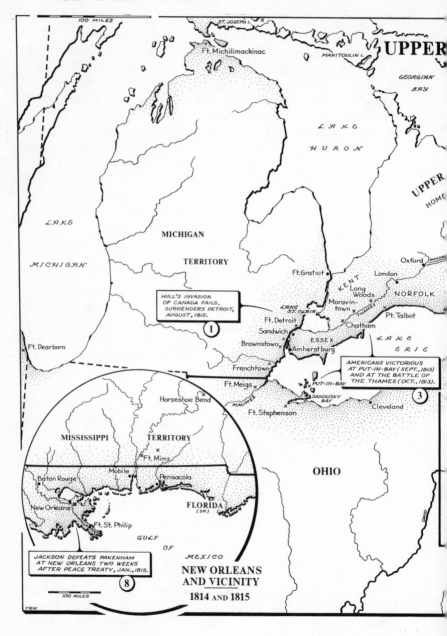

100 MILES

ST. JOSEPH I.

Ft. Michilimackinac

MANITOULIN I.

UPPER

GEORGIAN BAY

LAKE HURON

LAKE MICHIGAN

UPPER
HOME

MICHIGAN

TERRITORY

Ft. Gratiot

Oxford   DUNDA

London

KENT

NORFOLK

Long Woods

HULL'S INVASION OF CANADA FAILS, SURRENDERS DETROIT, AUGUST, 1812.

①

LAKE ST. CLAIR

Moravin-town

THAMES

Pt. Talbot

Ft. Detroit

Sandwich

Chatham

LAKE ERIE

Brownstown

ESSEX

Amherstburg

Ft. Dearborn

Frenchtown

AMERICANS VICTORIOUS AT PUT-IN-BAY (SEPT., 1813) AND AT THE BATTLE OF THE THAMES (OCT., 1813).

③

Ft. Meigs

PUT-IN-BAY

MAUMEE

SANDUSKY BAY

Horseshoe Bend

Ft. Stephenson

Cleveland

MISSISSIPPI   TERRITORY

Ft. Mims

Mobile

Pensacola

OHIO

Baton Rouge

New Orleans

FLORIDA (SP.)

Ft. St. Philip

GULF

OF

MEXICO

OHIO

JACKSON DEFEATS PAKENHAM AT NEW ORLEANS TWO WEEKS AFTER PEACE TREATY, JAN.,1815.

⑧

100 MILES

NEW ORLEANS AND VICINITY
1814 AND 1815

TRM

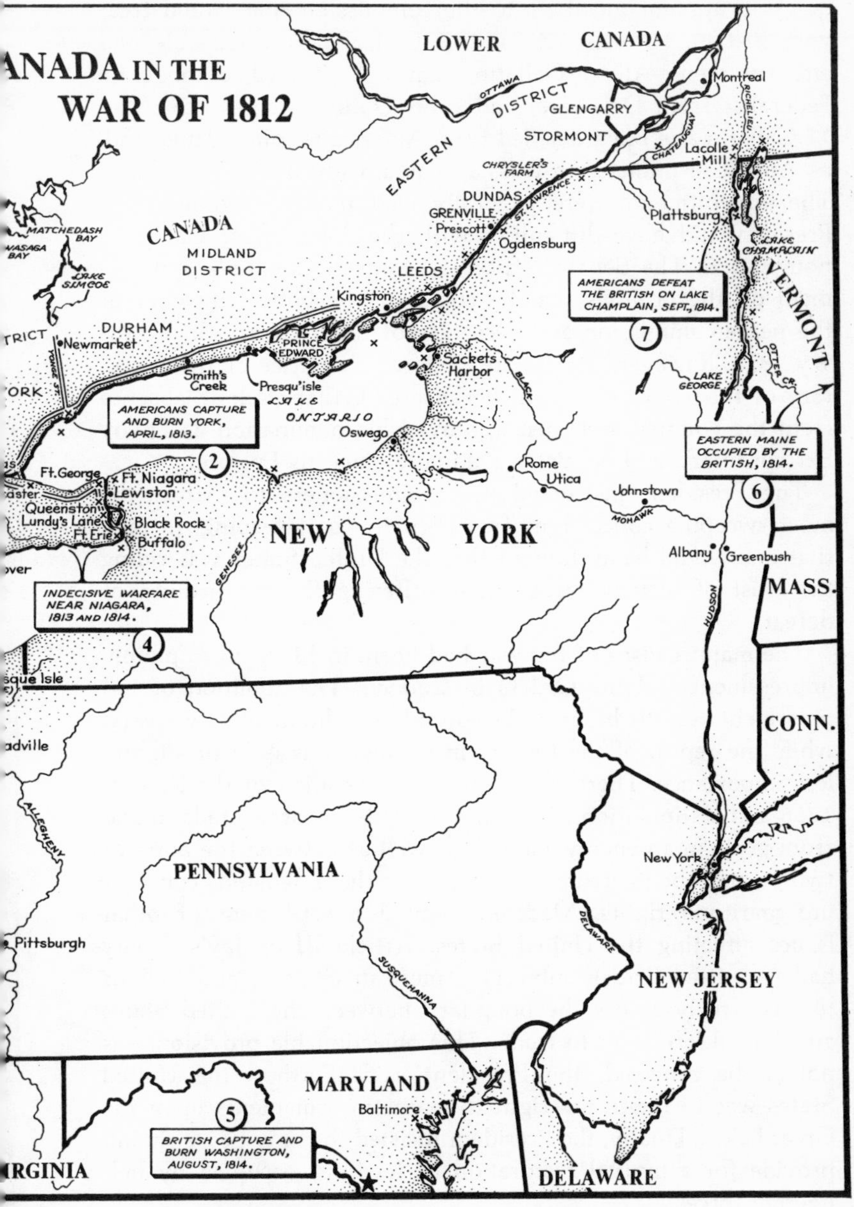

ANADA IN THE
WAR OF 1812
LOWER
CANADA
Montreal
OTTAWA
EASTERN DISTRICT
GLENGARRY
STORMONT
CHATEAUGUAY
RICHELIEU
Lacolle Mill
CHRYSLER'S FARM
DUNDAS
ST. LAWRENCE
GRENVILLE
Prescott
Ogdensburg
Plattsburg
LAKE CHAMPLAIN
VERMONT
CANADA
MATCHEDASH BAY
NASAGA BAY
LAKE SIMCOE
MIDLAND DISTRICT
LEEDS
Kingston
AMERICANS DEFEAT THE BRITISH ON LAKE CHAMPLAIN, SEPT., 1814.
7
TRICT
DURHAM
Newmarket
YONGE ST.
PRINCE EDWARD
Sackets Harbor
Smith's Creek
Presqu'isle
ORK
LAKE ONTARIO
BLACK
LAKE GEORGE
OTTER CR.
AMERICANS CAPTURE AND BURN YORK, APRIL, 1813.
Oswego
EASTERN MAINE OCCUPIED BY THE BRITISH, 1814.
2
Rome
Utica
Johnstown
MOHAWK
6
Ft. George
Ft. Niagara
Lewiston
Queenston
Lundy's Lane
Black Rock
Ft. Erie
Buffalo
NEW YORK
GENESEE
Albany
Greenbush
HUDSON
MASS.
INDECISIVE WARFARE NEAR NIAGARA, 1813 AND 1814.
4
sque Isle
adville
CONN.
ALLEGHENY
PENNSYLVANIA
New York
Pittsburgh
DELAWARE
SUSQUEHANNA
NEW JERSEY
MARYLAND
Baltimore
5
BRITISH CAPTURE AND BURN WASHINGTON, AUGUST, 1814.
IRGINIA
DELAWARE

quick to appoint members to the commission that would treat with Britain. He selected for this critical task three able and eminent men—Albert Gallatin, James A. Bayard, a moderate Federalist from Delaware, and John Quincy Adams. On May 11 Gallatin and Bayard sailed from America to join Adams who, as American minister to Russia, was already in St. Petersburg. The appointments were generally well received although the President did have difficulties with the Senate over Gallatin's nomination. The Senate refused to confirm Gallatin's appointment on the grounds that he could not be both a member of the peace commission and Secretary of the Treasury. In February 1814, however, the Senate declared the office of the Secretary of the Treasury vacant because of Gallatin's long absence from the country and then approved his nomination as Envoy Extraordinary and Minister Plenipotentiary to England.

The President instructed his commissioners to extract the most sweeping concessions from Britain—so sweeping, in fact, that one would have thought that the United States was riding the crest of victory rather than suffering the misfortunes of defeat.

The major causes of the war had been, in Madison's opinion, impressment and the Orders in Council. The abolition of impressment was to be an indispensable condition of any treaty, while the repeal of the Orders in Council was only of slightly less importance. There was to be a renunciation of the Rule of 1756 and a stipulation permitting neutrals to carry goods to and from ports in an enemy country as well as between the ports of two or more belligerents. In addition to these demands concerning maritime rights, Madison wanted a settlement of other issues affecting the United States. Article III of Jay's Treaty had permitted British subjects, American citizens, and Indians to pass freely across the boundary between the United States and Canada in order to trade. This objectionable provision was not to be renewed, the President said. Further, the United States was to retain the right to maintain armaments upon the Great Lakes. Finally, the President insisted that any peace should provide for a mutual restoration of territory occupied by belligerent forces.

With the exception of the last stipulation, these demands

were sharp and unlikely to be granted by Britain. Nevertheless, new demands were soon added to the charge sheet. Success had recently greeted American arms in Upper Canada. In April 1813 American troops had seized, burned, and looted York, the capital of Upper Canada, and had driven up the Niagara peninsula. Although they occupied York for only four days and were soon forced to retire from the peninsula, Monroe was greatly heartened by their performance. He felt that the scales were tipping in America's favor. Consequently, he ordered his commissioners to work for a settlement of the boundary through the Great Lakes to the Lake of the Woods. And because he hoped that American troops might ultimately seize all of Upper Canada, he suggested that Britain transfer this province to the United States. He realized that England would probably resist such a proposal, but he hoped that she might be convinced of its wisdom. By agreeing to it, he said, she would rid herself of a constant source of friction with the United States and would lift a continuous and heavy financial and military burden from her shoulders.

The American commissioners arrived at St. Petersburg on July 21, 1813. During the two months in which they had been traveling, Britain had been informed of the Tsar's offer of mediation and had rejected it. Adams had had an early intimation of London's reaction on June 7, 1813, when he had read in the English newspapers that the British government would probably reject the offer of mediation. Later in June he met with Count Romanzoff who told him that England's differences with the United States were, in the words of the British minister to Russia, "of a nature *involving principles of the internal government of the British nation* . . . which it was thought were not susceptible of being committed to the discussion of any mediation." [13] On July 14 Castlereagh wrote to Lord Cathcart, Britain's representative at the Tsar's headquarters, concerning the importance of "excluding from the general negotiations every maritime question." Great Britain, he said, "may be driven out of Congress, but not out of her maritime rights, and if the

---

[13] Adams to the Secretary of State, June 26, 1813, *American State Papers, Foreign Relations*, III, 627.

Continental Powers know their own interests, they will not hazard this." As an alternative to mediation by a third party, he suggested direct negotiations, either in London or, if that could not be managed, in Gothenburg.[14] This suggestion was received by Cathcart in August and was promptly communicated to the Tsar. Unfortunately, Alexander was slow in conveying its substance to Adams, for he hoped that Britain might change her mind. He was foolish to entertain such a notion, and he thus not only embarrassed Adams who suspected that his task was impossible but also puzzled Castlereagh who could not understand why the Americans remained in Russia. In November the British Foreign Minister sent to Washington an offer of direct negotiations. Madison received the proposal in December and, in the absence of news from Russia, he accepted it.

Britain's rejection of Russia's offer of mediation should have come as no surprise to Madison. It should have been apparent to the President that Britain would not submit so vital an issue as impressment to a negotiation presided over by a third party. Adams felt that Britain's reaction to Alexander's offer was perfectly understandable. "The fear," he wrote, "of complicating the maritime question between Britain and America with the general politics of Europe is just and rational on the part of England." [15] In addition to this legitimate concern, Britain felt a profound anger toward the United States. America's declaration of war had deprived British troops in the Iberian Peninsula campaign of much-needed supplies and had made their military operations more difficult. Further, many felt that America had struck a dangerous blow at Britain at a critical moment in her history. As a consequence, Britain was in no mood to place her future in the hands of a mediator. She was, however, prepared for a direct confrontation with American negotiators, and so the stage was set for the discussions that led to the final treaty.

---

[14] Lord Castlereagh to Lord Cathcart, July 14, 1813, W. Vane, Marquess of Londonderry (ed.), *Correspondence, Despatches and Other Papers of Viscount Castlereagh* (13 vols., London, 1852), VIII, 34–35.

[15] J. Q. Adams to John Adams, September 3, 1813, W. C. Ford (ed.), *The Writings of John Quincy Adams* (7 vols., New York, 1914), IV, 515.

The decision to open direct negotiations with Britain led to the appointment of a new commission acting under new instructions. This group, as first constituted, included John Quincy Adams, James A. Bayard, Jonathan Russell, and Henry Clay. Clay was to represent Western interests with the same kind of passion and dedication that he had brought to the Congressional struggle for war. Albert Gallatin, through an error, was at first left out of the commission, but this mistake was soon rectified. It was fortunate that it was, for he brought to the deliberations a calm wisdom that was to prove essential to its success.

The new instructions to the American commissioners were issued on January 28, 1814. The negotiators were, in general, to follow the instructions given earlier to Adams, Bayard, and Gallatin, but Madison and Monroe wished to extract further concessions from Britain. As before, Britain was expected to give up impressment. This "degrading" practice, the President wrote, must cease, for "our flag must protect the crew, or the United States cannot consider themselves an independent nation." But in addition to agreeing to the abolition of this practice, England was to pay all impressed Americans, upon their discharge, the wages that they might otherwise have earned in the merchant service. This payment would have amounted to a formidable sum of money, and no matter how desirable it might have been in the interests of justice, the harsh facts of reality would prevent it from being made. Again, the commissioners were urged to secure a more precise and favorable definition of blockades. And again, there was an article on indemnities, but this time it was expanded so that the United States would receive payment for "the destruction of all unfortified towns, and other private property contrary to the laws and usages of war . . . ." The return of, or full payment for, all Negroes taken from the South was also asked.

These instructions might be considered the product of an overvaulting ambition. But they did not stop there. Monroe wanted the commissioners to work for the cession of Canada. This had always been a desirable goal, but the war had made it seem doubly necessary. Experience had shown, wrote Monroe, "that the British Government cannot participate in the domination and navigation of the Lakes, without incurring the danger of an early renewal of the war." It was by means of the Great Lakes, he continued,

. . . that the British Government interfered with and gained an ascendency over the Indians, even within our own limits. The effect produced by the massacre of our citizens after they were made prisoners, and of defenseless women and children along our frontier need not be described. It will perhaps never be removed while Great Britain retains in her hands the government of those provinces.

But control of the Indians was not the only reason why America desired Canada. The rapid expansion of America's frontier raised problems that could be solved, Monroe felt, only through annexation. The westward movement of pioneers would soon fill the areas south of the Great Lakes with Americans. When this happened, the Secretary of State said, "collisions may be daily expected between the inhabitants on each side, which it may not be in the power of either Government to prevent." As the inevitable consequence of another war, he continued, "must be to sever these provinces by force from Great Britain," it would be the better part of wisdom to arrange their peaceful transfer to America now.[16] Some months later Monroe instructed the commissioners to insist upon the return of Fort Astor on the Columbia River to the United States. At the beginning of the war that lonely American outpost had been hastily sold by the Astor Company to the Northwest Company before it could be seized by British forces. It was now the wish of the United States to set aside this transaction because, as Monroe said, "it is not believed that they [the British] have any claim whatever to territory on the Pacific Ocean." [17] This was a disputable point and was to lead later to a crisis over Oregon, which placed a heavy strain on Anglo-American relations.

The demands set forth by Washington were impossible of fulfillment. As so often in the past, the United States had asked for terms which neither her power nor situation justified. And

[16] Donnan, *Annual Report of the American Historical Association,* 1913, 263–264.
[17] The Secretary of State to the American Plenipotentiaries, March 22, 1814, *American State Papers, Foreign Relations,* III, 731.

again, as so often in the past, she hoped that the skill of her negotiators would gloss over the weakness of her case. But America was bound to be disappointed. Only one of two conditions would give the American aspirations substance and hope. Either Britain would have to be soundly defeated in Canada, or she would have to be desperately engaged in Europe. Neither of these conditions existed. British troops were pressed in Canada, but they were in no danger of being expelled from that country. And England's prospects in Europe had never been brighter. Indeed, with the aid of Prussia, she was closing in upon Napoleon and in April had forced his abdication in Paris and his exile to Elba.

The imminent defeat of France should have sobered the American administration, for Britain would soon be free to move substantial forces to Canada. But Washington was a city of eternal optimism, and the prospect of future adversity did not, at first, modify the administration's position. Although it was decided in cabinet meetings on June 23 and 24 that impressment might become the subject of separate negotiations after a peace was signed, the dispatch to the peace commissioners conveying this information added a new dimension to their task. Adams and his colleagues were now told that under no circumstances were they to surrender America's fishing privileges. Indeed, said Monroe, they were not even to discuss the problem; if the British insisted on doing so, the negotiations were to be terminated immediately.

Several days after these instructions were sent, the problem of impressment was reviewed at another cabinet meeting. This time the meeting was a more somber affair, for the President had just received news from Bayard and Gallatin of the disasters that were encompassing Napoleon. If Britain would not give up impressment when she was beleaguered, was she likely to surrender it in the flush of victory? The answer was self-evident. If a peace were to be negotiated, the whole issue of impressment would have to be shelved. Fortunately, the defeat of France would make the subject an academic one in any case. And so the President instructed his representatives to conclude a peace without reference to one of the major causes of the war. He could do nothing else; although some have criticized

his actions, how much more serious would be the charges
against him if he had prolonged the war by doggedly insisting
that impressment be settled. But this step did not sufficiently
lighten the burden of the commissioners. Their demands were
still too heavy, and their prospects for success were still dark.
Adams privately admitted that the negotiations would be of
"long continuance." [18] If he had known the extent of Britain's
requirements, he would have been even more depressed, for
they were to be as extreme as America's.

Any treaty, to be acceptable to England, would have to
leave her maritime principles untouched. It would also have to
secure Canada from any future attack and rectify the mistakes
made in the earlier settlements of 1783 and 1794. The error made
when the Indians were forsaken in 1783 was to be remedied
by the creation of an Indian barrier state. The existence of
this state was to be jointly guaranteed by both powers, and its
boundaries were to follow those of the Treaty of Greenville.
The size of this area was startling, for it included the bulk of
the present states of Ohio, Illinois, Michigan, Indiana, and
Wisconsin. This neutralized area would, it was felt, protect the
Indians from new encroachments by the white settlers and,
equally important, secure the upper reaches of Canada from
future American aggression. So important was the attainment
of these objectives to Britain that she made the article on the
buffer state a *sine qua non* of any treaty. Britain's other demands were no less exacting than the first. Article III of Jay's
Treaty was to be renewed. The boundary of British North
America was to be revised in order to obtain security from
future attack and to remove the cause of existing border disputes. The islands of Passamaquoddy Bay were to be British;
the boundary of Maine was to be lowered to the 47th parallel
in order to provide for safe communications between New
Brunswick and Quebec; and Britain's route through the Great
Lakes was to be protected by the cession of both Michilimackinac and a strip of land on the east side of the Niagara River. A
clause barring American warships from the Great Lakes was

---

[18] J. Q. Adams to L. Adams, August 9, 1814, Ford, *The Writings of John
Quincy Adams*, IV, 74.

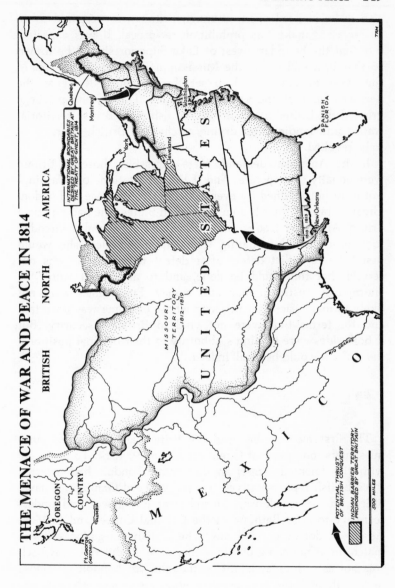

THE MENACE OF WAR AND PEACE IN 1814

BRITISH   NORTH   AMERICA

OREGON
COUNTRY

Ft. George
(ASTORIA)

COLUMBIA

Quebec

Montreal

INTERNATIONAL BOUNDARIES
DESIRED BY GREAT BRITAIN AT
THE TREATY OF GHENT, 1814

Washington

New York

Cleveland

OHIO

UNITED   STATES

MISSOURI
TERRITORY
1812–1810

RIO GRANDE

M   E   X   I   C   O

New Orleans

SPANISH
FLORIDA

POTENTIAL THRUST
OF BRITISH CONQUEST

INDIAN BARRIER TERRITORY
PROPOSED BY GREAT BRITAIN

500 MILES

also to be insisted upon, although Britain was prepared to go so far as to make this prohibition reciprocal. It was expected, too, that the boundary west of Lake Superior should be drawn so that it would strike the Mississippi River at its source. In the West Britain wished to set the Columbia River as the northern limit of the Oregon Territory. Finally, the privilege granted the United States in 1783 of fishing in British territorial waters and landing and drying catches on British shores was to be revoked.

If the American demands were excessive, those of Britain were equally intemperate. And if the expectations of Washington were not justified by events, neither were those of London. Great Britain had not beaten the United States; she had not even driven American troops from Canada. If she really intended to impose such humiliating terms upon America, she would first have to inflict defeat after defeat upon her. It was not certain that this could be done, and to attempt it would be enormously costly in men and money. Englishmen were not likely to make sacrifices in a war whose outcome was uncertain and for terms that were not vital to Britain's security. But if both sides were to cling stubbornly to their original positions, the outlook would be bleak indeed.

The first meeting between the British and American commissioners took place at Ghent on August 9, 1814. To negotiate with the talented American delegation London had selected three British representatives. They were Lord Gambier, a naval officer, Henry Goulburn, a member of Parliament and under-secretary to Lord Bathurst at the Colonial Office, and William Adams, a doctor of civil law. The British delegation did not match the American group in ability or skill. But this drawback was not as serious as might be thought, for London was close to Ghent, and the British representatives could refer all important matters back to the cabinet for decision. America, on the other hand, because of her great distance from Europe, had to appoint men who were prepared to use their best judgment and to depart from the letter of their instructions if the interests of their country would be served by their doing so.

At the first session the tone of the meetings was established. They were to be long, frequently acrimonious, and often tiresome. Each side would attempt to wring the maximum concessions from the other. Each would press legalistic arguments to buttress its case, and each would insist that national security required a surrender of vital interests by the other. Of course, neither party would get what it wanted. A diplomatic triumph is seldom achieved by powers engaged in a war that neither really wishes to fight to a bitter and costly finish. Nevertheless, both countries persisted in the belief that forceful presentations of their cases could secure what military power was unable to obtain.

The British delegates first put forward Castlereagh's points for discussion. The point dealing with maritime rights was quickly shelved because, as Adams observed, the British *"intimated"* that their government was not *"desirous"* of discussing it. Before continuing the talks, the British asked whether the Americans were empowered to treat upon the remaining topics. The Americans admitted that although they had instructions to deal with the revision of the boundary, they were not authorized to discuss the Indian barrier state or the fisheries. Indeed, they said, since these points "had not been the object of controversy between the two governments heretofore . . . it could not be expected that they should have been anticipated by the government of the United States." Peace with the Indians, they continued, was considered to be an "inevitable consequence of peace with Great Britain." Further, the proposition to give the Indians a distinct boundary was not only new and unexampled but also unnecessary, for commissioners had already been appointed by Washington to make peace with them.[19]

After hearing this answer, the British asked whether any provisional agreement could be reached on these subjects. The Americans replied that they were willing to discuss any topic but pointed out that their government had not authorized them to deal with certain subjects and that Washington could not

---

[19] Adams to the Secretary of State, August 11, 1814, Ford, *ibid.*, V, 75–82.

therefore be bound by any accommodation that they might make. Goulburn was not satisfied with this answer, although it was the most that he could have in conscience expected. He promptly wrote to London asking whether he should proceed to negotiate an Indian settlement that might be rejected by Madison. Castlereagh's reply nearly ended all hopes of a treaty then and there, for he insisted that the Indian barrier state be considered indispensable to any settlement. He did soften the harshness of his position somewhat by saying that he was prepared to accept the Treaty of Greenville as the basis for negotiations, but this was small comfort to the American delegation. The irritation felt by the Americans over the Indian issue turned into high indignation when they learned of Castlereagh's other demands—that the southern shore of the Great Lakes be demilitarized, that the free navigation of the Mississippi be ensured, and that a direct line of communication between Quebec and Halifax be secured.

Adams exploded with anger when these terms were presented. Our opponents, he cried, are "charged fourfold with obnoxious substance . . . ." [20] Further conversation with the British delegation convinced him that he had been conservative in his judgment, for the British brushed off all protests with an infuriating blandness. When Gallatin asked what was to become of the one hundred thousand Americans now living within the projected Indian buffer state, he was simply told that some of them would be taken care of in subsequent boundary adjustments, and that the rest would have to shift for themselves. When he inquired about the disposition of Moose Island, he was calmly informed that all the islands in Passamaquoddy Bay belonged to Britain. When Bayard suggested that the western boundary should run from the Lake of the Woods, he was quickly told that it should not be drawn from there but rather from the western tip of Lake Superior. Finally, to complete the exercise in frustration, the British delegates informed the Americans that should this conference be broken off while new instructions were sought from the United States, Britain would feel "at liberty to vary and regulate her demands ac-

---

[20] J. Q. Adams to L. Adams, Ford, *ibid.*, IV, 90.

cording to subsequent events, and in such manner as the state of the war, at the time of renewing the negotiations, might warrant." [21]

This unpleasant meeting both shocked and outraged the Americans. They were furious at the demands of the British, which they deemed unreasonable and unwarranted either by simple justice or by the state of hostilities. Indeed, their written answer to the British proposals was couched in such sharp and penetrating language that none of them expected the negotiations to continue. They rejected an Indian barrier state carved out of American territory and denounced the proposal to revise the boundary of 1783. They were contemptuous of the suggestion that they give up the right of maintaining naval forces on the Great Lakes. They insisted that such dishonorable terms, if accepted, could lead only to a temporary truce, for at the first opportunity the United States would take up arms to undo a humiliating peace. Angered as they were by the British proposals, however, the Americans did not want to close the door completely. They had come to Ghent, they said, to end the war on a basis of honorable reciprocity. They therefore suggested that the British agree to a treaty which would provide for a simple restoration of conquered territory, but which would also reserve for each party all its rights concerning its seamen.

After delivering this sharply worded note, the Americans began to prepare for their departure. They had no expectation that Britain would recede from her extravagant position, and they had no desire to retreat from their own stand. Madison, knowing of their dilemma, wrote that he expected them to leave Ghent shortly. Goulburn was equally pessimistic, and he informed Bathurst that the Americans did not mean to continue the negotiations. Only Britain could save the situation. The United States had now conceded all that she could. She had offered to waive the issue of neutral rights and to accept the boundary as it existed before the declaration of war. She could do no more. But if Britain did not match this spirit of conciliation, the talks would collapse and the war would drag on, with

---

[21] Adams, Bayard, Clay, Russell and Gallatin to Monroe, August 19, 1814, *American State Papers, Foreign Relations*, III, 708–709.

the possibility of future accommodation becoming even more difficult.

It was clearly to Britain's interest to end a war from which she had so little to gain. And so the cabinet began its retreat. On August 28 the British Foreign Secretary wrote to Liverpool that the "substance of the question is, are we prepared to continue the war for territorial arrangements; . . . and if not, is this the best time to make our peace, saving all our rights and claiming the fisheries . . . or is it desirable to take the chance of the campaign, and then to be governed by circumstances?" It was his own view that it would be "imprudent" to fight the war for "territorial" principles. If Britain did, he thought that the action would only stimulate the Americans to even greater efforts and increase the unpopularity of the contest at home. If, on the other hand, Britain sought an immediate peace, he thought that the Americans might be prepared to sign a "Provisional article of Indian peace, as distinct from limits," and might be willing to relinquish claims to the islands in Passamaquoddy Bay. They might go so far as to agree to an adjustment of the boundary that would secure a line of communication from Quebec to Halifax.[22]

Castlereagh's opinion was shared by the Prime Minister. Little could be done about the frontier, he felt, and "military events must decide that question." But the other terms could be altered. He argued that the Indians would have to be included in the peace and he felt that it should restore to them all their "rights and privileges." However, if Prevost in Canada had promised them more than this, he was prepared to prolong the war. But he was not ready to go much beyond this point. He wanted to end the war, and he wanted to end it now. Goulburn and the other commissioners, he complained,

. . . evidently do not feel the inconveniences of the war. I feel it strongly, but I feel it is nothing now compared with what it may be a twelve-month hence, and I am particularly anxious therefore, that we should avoid anything . . . which may increase our difficulties in concluding it.[23]

---

[22] Castlereagh to Liverpool, August 28, 1814, Vane, *Correspondence, Despatches and Other Papers of Viscount Castlereagh*, X, 101–102.
[23] Liverpool to Bathurst, September 15, 1814, *Report on the Manuscripts of Earl Bathurst* (London, 1923), 288–289.

Liverpool's exhaustion with the war stemmed from his recognition that Britain had been fighting for nearly a generation and her people were tired of the strains of combat. He was also afraid that the economy might not rise above the stresses that a long and taxing war fought three thousand miles away would place upon it. His determination to offer reasonable terms in order to secure a peace was soon reflected in the attitude of the British commissioners at Ghent. In a note of September 19 they indicated a willingness to accept an article that simply "restored" to the Indians the "rights, privileges and territories which they enjoyed in the year 1811 . . . ." They also said that the exclusive military possession of the Great Lakes had never been "considered a *sine qua non* in the negotiation," and that they were now prepared to make a "final disposition on the subject of Canadian boundaries, so entirely founded on the principles of moderation and justice, that they feel confident it cannot be rejected." [24]

The new propositions advanced by Britain encouraged the hope that a settlement could be reached, but the proposals could only serve as the starting point for discussions. Adams found the Indian article so offensive that he was prepared to break off the talks on its account alone. His colleagues prevailed upon him to temper his anger and to submit to the British a counterproposal on this vexatious and divisive issue. What the Americans suggested was simplicity itself. Both countries would merely agree that no citizens or Indians of either nation would be punished for any part that they might have played in the hostilities. If, Adams said, this article was not agreeable to Britain, it would at least have the merit of bringing the discussions "to a point which will prevent further dilatory proceedings." [25]

Adams's expectation was quickly realized; although Britain rejected this proposal, she offered a reasonable alternative in its place. She now suggested that the Indians be simply restored to the rights and privileges that they had enjoyed in 1811.

---

[24] The British Commissioners to the American Commissioners, September 19, 1814, *American State Papers, Foreign Relations*, III, 717–718.

[25] J. Q. Adams to L. Adams, Ford, *The Writings of John Quincy Adams*, V, 146.

This was a far cry from a barrier state, but it was a proposition that the United States might accept. Since Bathurst felt
strongly that the Indians should secure some guarantee of their
future security, he persuaded Liverpool to submit it as an ultimatum. The Prime Minister agreed to this, not only because he
shared Bathurst's views on the subject but also because news
of a recent military success in North America made him feel
that the Americans would now be in a more amenable frame
of mind. In July 1814, a British army of Wellington's veterans
had routed the American forces at Bladensburg with ridiculous
ease, entered Washington, put the torch to its military installa-
tions and governmental offices, and then retired to a fleet
waiting offshore. The destruction of York in 1813 had been
repaid. The effects of this striking victory were diminished by
the defeat inflicted upon British forces when they attempted
to mete out the same treatment to Baltimore. Nevertheless,
London was cheered by the turn of events in America, and
Bathurst wrote the British commissioners instructing them to
tell the American delegates about the victory at Washington.
He also asked them to inform the Americans that Britain would
not let this intelligence from America affect her attitude to
boundary revisions unless the United States rejected the Indian
article.

It is always disagreeable to negotiate under duress. Adams,
although admitting that the British proposal was not couched
in its usual domineering style, still preferred to break off talks
than to accept it. But neither Gallatin nor Bayard saw anything
sufficiently sinister in the new offer to justify such a step. They
persuaded Adams to accept the proposal, but he wrung a
promise from them that they would surrender nothing of importance in the future. The need for this assurance stemmed
not from a distrust in the ability of his colleagues but from his
knowledge that matters close to his heart would soon arise.
These would include the fisheries, and Adams wanted a united
delegation to fight for them.

The American acceptance of the Indian article cleared the
way for a final peace treaty. It was still to prove difficult to
gain, but it was no longer impossible. Adams and his associates
now asked Britain to send them the project of a treaty. Bathurst

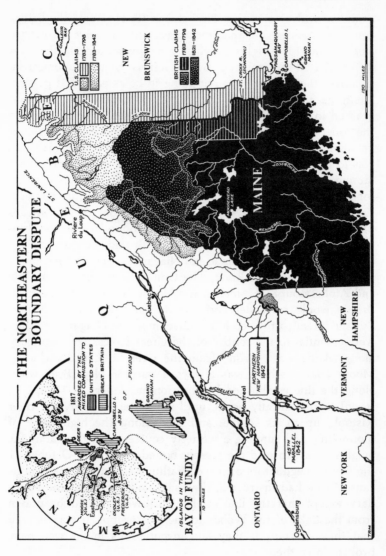

THE NORTHEASTERN
BOUNDARY DISPUTE

complied with this request on October 18. He wrote the British commissioners saying that the agreement to waive all discussions on maritime rights provided a happy solution to the most difficult of all the problems. But he warned that an accommodation over the fisheries was not going to be as easy. His government, he insisted, could not "agree to renew the privilege, granted in 1783, and annulled by the present war of allowing the Americans to land and dry their fish on the unsettled shores belonging to his Britannic Majesty. . . ." The boundary question was to be settled, he continued, on the basis of each power retaining territory it now controlled, subject only to "modification for mutual accommodation." He then enumerated the modifications but ordered that they be withheld from the Americans until they had promised to negotiate the boundary on the principle just stated (*uti possidetis*). Great Britain, he declared, occupied Forts Michilimackinac and Niagara as well as the country east of the Penobscot River. The United States held Forts Erie and Amherstburg. If America would return the posts she held, Britain would surrender Forts Castine and Machias in Maine. But she intended to keep Michilimackinac and Niagara, for they were essential to the control of the Great Lakes. The boundary along Maine was to run "from the river St. Croix, including Moose Island, which was always a part of New Brunswick, along the line established by the Commissioners in 1798, . . . [then] astronomically north, until it is intersected by the river Ristook, up to its source; and then along the high ridge of mountains, and running a westerly course, until they abut the heights which formed the present boundary." [26] On October 21 the British negotiators conveyed Bathurst's terms to the Americans. As he had instructed, they said nothing about the boundary except that the line in the Northwest should be drawn from the Lake of the Woods to the Mississippi. It was as well that they did not; if they had, negotiations might well have broken down then.

Bathurst had hardly sent his instructions to Ghent when the received disastrous news from North America. Britain had

[26] Lord Bathurst to the Commissioners at Ghent, October 18, 1814, Vane, *Correspondence, Despatches and Other Papers of Viscount Castlereagh,* X, 168–170.

planned to bring military pressure to bear upon the United States on several fronts. She had already attacked Washington and Baltimore, and she had made successful forays along the northeast coast of Maine. She had also planned an attack upon New Orleans. But her major and most damaging thrust was to be made down the Lake Champlain route into New York. In September 1814, Prevost led a powerful army down the shores of the lake, but his progress was halted and his advance turned into ignominious retreat when the British fleet was all but wiped out at Plattsburg. Without control of Lake Champlain, nothing could be ventured. This engagement was one of the truly decisive ones fought during the war, and its effects were felt both by the military planners in London and the negotiators at Ghent. After Plattsburg any projected invasion of the United States would have to be postponed until Britain regained control of Lake Champlain. And that would be a long time in coming because a new fleet would have to be built from scratch. Yet, curiously enough, the immediate news of this fiasco did not have the effect one might have expected. Bathurst seemed buoyed by the challenge of this disaster, and instead of modifying his stand, he hardened his attitude. He now seemed bent on the incredible course of presenting the boundary settlement as an ultimatum. Happily Liverpool was able to divert him from this reckless course, but not far enough, for Bathurst instructed the commissioners to draw the boundary line of Maine along the Passamaquoddy River to the 46th parallel and thence to the boundary of Lower Canada. They were also told that Britain now laid claim to Carleton Island; that she wanted the island of Michilimackinac as well as the fort; and that she needed not only Fort Niagara but also some five miles of territory surrounding it. These were preposterous terms which should never have been asked, for agreement could never have been reached on them.

Fortunately, slow communications prevented these proposals from reaching the Americans before they had answered the note of October 21. As it was, their reply to the earlier British terms was sharp enough. They categorically refused to treat on the basis of *uti possidetis* or any principle that would involve the cession of American territory. They were prepared to continue negotiations only if it was agreed that there would be a mutual restoration of territory. If the British would agree to this, the Americans said, they would be happy to receive a treaty *project* from them. It appeared that an impasse, similar to the one over the Indians, was near. But events were soon to compel Britain to accept the American terms. Adams had thought that only military defeats in North America or danger and confusion in Europe would deflect Britain from her course. His premonition was soon confirmed. Tsar Alexander of Russia fostered an ambition to restore Poland and make himself its king, and his intrigue rapidly divided the allies into two camps. Liverpool's capacity to deal forcefully with this situation was inhibited by Britain's entanglement in America. And so the Prime Minister began to reduce his demands at Ghent. Before he did so, however, he talked to Wellington, for he had nurtured the hope that Wellington might go to Canada to bring the war to a swift and successful conclusion. But Wellington told him that "matters are in so uncomfortable a state here [Europe] and they are so little settled in Congress [Vienna] that you could not spare me out of Europe. . . ." [27] Several days later, Wellington wrote Liverpool a letter that strengthened the Prime Minister's growing conviction that the war should be ended in America and that it should be concluded on terms very similar to those offered by the United States. "I confess that I think you have no right," Wellington said, "from the state of the war to demand any concession from America." He continued:

Considering everything, it is my opinion that the war has been a most successful one, and highly honourable to the British arms; but from particular circumstances, such as the want of the naval superiority on the Lakes, you have not been able to carry it into the enemy's territory, notwithstanding your military success, and now undoubtedly military superiority, and have not even cleared your own territory of the enemy on the point of attack. You cannot then, on any principle of equality in negotiation, claim a cession of territory excepting in exchange for other advantages which you have in your power. . . . Then if all this reasoning be true, why stipulate for the *uti possidetis?*

---

[27] Wellington to Bathurst, November 4, 1814, *Report on the Manuscripts of Earl Bathurst*, 303.

You can get no territory; indeed the state of your military operations, however creditable, does not entitle you to demand any.[28]

Liverpool's change in policy led to a quickening in the tempo of negotiations. On November 10 the American commissioners sent the draft of a treaty to the British negotiators. It consisted of fifteen articles of which the first seven, the ninth, the fifteenth, and an additional one on the slave trade were to form the substance of the final Treaty of Ghent. Articles I and II of the American draft called for the establishment of a "firm and universal peace" and restoration "without delay" of all "territory, places and possessions" seized by either party during hostilities. Articles III to VI provided for the settlement of outstanding boundary disputes. Commissions were to be established to decide the ownership of Grand Manan Island as well as the islands in Passamaquoddy Bay; to locate accurately "the northwest angle of Nova Scotia" and the "northwesternmost head of the Connecticut river and to survey the line between these two points; to draw the line properly in the waterway through the St. Lawrence River and the Great Lakes so that the islands there could be rightly apportioned; to do the same for the boundary from Lake Superior to the Lake of the Woods; and to have those stretches of the boundary that required it "surveyed and marked." Article VII of the draft provided for the regulation of the commissions. Article VIII proposed that the boundary west of the Lake of the Woods be drawn from the northwestern point of the lake due north or south until it struck the 49th parallel and thence due west. Article IX contained the agreement already reached concerning the Indians, and Article X proposed that each power "restrain the Indians living within their respective dominions from committing hostilities" against the other. It also suggested that each power promise never to use the Indians in any future war. Articles XI, XII, and XIII concerned impressment, blockades, and indemnities for losses. Article XIV provided for a general amnesty, and Article XV for ratification.[29]

---

[28] Wellington to Liverpool, November 9, 1814, Ford, *The Writings of John Quincy Adams*, V, 179, n. 2.

[29] *American State Papers, Foreign Relations*, III, 735–740.

Missing from the treaty *projet* was an article on the fisheries. It was omitted because the American delegation was dangerously—nearly fatally—split on the matter. Gallatin had prepared an article providing for the renewal of the American privilege of fishing in British inshore waters and the British privilege of navigating on the Mississippi River. He had linked these two topics for two basic reasons. First, both privileges had a common origin in the Treaty of 1783. And second and more important, London had made it quite clear that the fishing privileges would not be granted again unless some equivalent were offered, and the only one that the United States held in its hand was the free navigation of the Mississippi. Clay, however, was violently opposed to granting this concession to Britain. He wanted to exclude her from the Mississippi River, and he was more than willing to sacrifice the fishing privileges in order to accomplish this. Adams was equally unyielding in his view that the fisheries must be protected. So contentious was this dispute in the American delegation, and so wholly divergent were the views expressed by Clay and Adams, that a compromise had to be found. They finally agreed to insert in the treaty not an article but rather a simple statement to the effect that, because of the unique character of the Treaty of 1783, the United States was entitled to enjoy the fishing liberties she had received with her independence.

The treaty *projet* was then sent to Britain. On November 21 Bathurst returned a revised version to the Americans. The articles concerning the use of Indians in war, impressment, blockade, indemnities, and a general amnesty were deemed inadmissible. The remaining articles were accepted with little change. Instead of the three members for the boundary commissions proposed by the United States, Bathurst suggested only two. If these commissioners could not reach agreement, the dispute would be arbitrated by a friendly and independent sovereign. And he proposed that the article defining the boundary west of the Lake of the Woods include a provision giving British subjects free access to the Mississippi River and free navigation upon it.

The British proposals were received by the American plenipotentiaries with every evidence of pleasure. The last great ob-

stacle to peace had been removed with the agreement to sign a
treaty based upon the principle of the *status quo ante bellum.*
As Adams said, although the British have rejected "without exception everything we have demanded on the part of the United
States . . . they had abandoned everything that was inadmissible
of their own demands." As a consequence, he continued, "The
objects upon which they still insist, and which we cannot yield,
are in themselves so trifling and insignificant that neither of the
two nations would tolerate a war for them. We have everything
but peace in our hands." [30]

Peace was soon to come, but not before there was give and
take on both sides. The main stumbling block to a final treaty
lay in the fisheries and the navigation of the Mississippi River.
There were other differences, but these were easily disposed of.
The Americans agreed to delete from the treaty all the articles
concerning maritime rights, and they reluctantly agreed also to
forego compensation for their merchant vessels seized in British
ports at the outbreak of the war. But the fisheries and the
Mississippi River proved to be more difficult subjects. Britain's
determination to keep America out of the fisheries (unless
granted an adequate equivalent) and Clay's determination to
keep England out of the Mississippi prolonged the negotiations.
Proposals from the United States were answered by counter-
proposals from Great Britain. The interminable exchange of
notes proved only that agreement on the terms desired by either
side was impossible. There were two alternatives. Either the
talks would have to be broken off, or both sides would have to
compromise. Since it would have been unthinking folly to continue a war when a peace could be reached by the exercise of
wisdom and restraint, an agreement was struck. The treaty
would contain no reference to the navigation of the Mississippi
River or to the fisheries. The last obstacle to a settlement had
been hurdled. On December 23 the final draft of the treaty was
agreed to, and on the day before Christmas it was signed.
Prompt ratification followed.

Thus, after weeks of arduous negotiating and months of

---

[30] J. Q. Adams to L. Adams, November 29, 1814, Ford, *The Writings of
John Quincy Adams,* V, 219.

fighting, peace came. Despite all the talk about absolute positions from which there could be no retreat, the settlement finally reached was largely a negative one. All questions relating to impressment, blockades, contraband, and the Rule of 1756 were ignored. The Indian barrier state was dropped. The fisheries and the boundary west of Lake of the Woods were left to future negotiations. Even the navigation of the Mississippi River and the problems connected with Article III of Jay's Treaty concerning Indian trade were left unresolved. The new treaty simply provided for the cessation of hostilities and the establishment of mixed commissions to settle certain boundary disputes.

Yet it would be wrong to suggest that because the Treaty of Ghent made no mention of neutral rights, the United States had submitted to British maritime practices. American opposition to these practices was quite as strong in 1814 as it had been in 1812. But the defeat of Napoleon had automatically put an end to these abrasive practices; as they no longer existed in fact, Washington did not feel constrained to fight for their abolition in the future. However, the United States made it known that a renewal of impressment would be vigorously resisted. If Britain, Jefferson wrote,

. . . thinks the exercise of this outrage is worth eternal war, eternal war it must be, or extermination of the one or other party. The first act of impressment she commits on an American, will be answered by reprisal, or by a declaration of war here. . . .[31]

It was felt that Britain's knowledge of this would restrain her from committing future acts of aggression. It would have been preferable to have a clause written into the treaty, but the United States believed that her actions in 1812 would serve to guarantee her security in the years ahead. This is why Adams could write with conviction that he had signed a settlement which had "surrendered no right of the nation . . . ."[32]

Britain, too, had no reason to be disappointed with the treaty. She had preserved the theoretical right to use her maritime

---

[31] Jefferson to Lafayette, February 14, 1815, Lipscomb and Bergh (eds.), *The Writings of Thomas Jefferson*, XIV, 254–255.

[32] J. Q. Adams to L. Adams, Ford, *The Writings of John Quincy Adams*, V, 261.

measures in the future if their application were deemed vital to the preservation of her security. She had also gained a formal stipulation that recognized and guaranteed the rights of the Indians. Although she had not been able to gain agreement to any demilitarization of the Great Lakes, she could comfort herself with the knowledge that Canada was reasonably secure from future military aggression. Adams said as much during the negotiations when he observed that any American attack upon the British provinces in North America would condemn the Atlantic seaboard of the United States to a destructive attack by the Royal Navy. As important to the safety of Canada as this understanding was the provision in the treaty for the amicable means of settling disputes involving Canada. The creation of commissions for arbitrating differences was not new in international affairs, but the extensive use of them called for at Ghent was surely unparalleled in history.

But the War of 1812 had a significance reaching far beyond the terms of the treaty that concluded it. To Great Britain it was a minor affair which only served to divert some of her resources from the major conflict she was waging with France. To the United States it was much more. America had entered it to defend her vital interests, uphold her national honor, and assert her newly won independence. War is the harshest test to which a nation can be put. And the United States found it doubly hazardous in 1812, for she had entered the conflict with a divided Congress and a confused citizenry. Yet despite the uncertainty that plagued the nation, she was able to meet the challenge with honor. Though she had suffered military reverses, and though the Hartford Convention called in New England in 1814 heard men talk of secession rather than fighting, these disasters and divisions were forgotten when the war was ended. Indeed, a sense of buoyancy swept the country in 1815 when news of Andrew Jackson's victory at New Orleans was received. That the engagement took place two weeks after the Treaty of Ghent was signed and that it did not have any effect upon the terms of this peace were circumstances that most people chose to ignore. Instead, the nation saw it as a vindication of American honor and triumph of American arms.

And so the United States emerged from the war with a new

sense of purpose and identity. Shortly after the end of hostilities, Albert Gallatin wrote:

The War has been productive of evil and good, but I think that the good preponderates .... The War renewed and reinstated the National feelings and character which the revolution had given, and which were daily lessened. The people now have more general objects of attachment with which their pride and political opinions are connected. They are more American: they feel and act more as a Nation, and I hope that the permanency of the Union is thereby better secured.[33]

Gallatin was right; the nation was better able to face the future. There were still foreign problems to deal with, but the actions that the United States had taken in 1812 made their resolution easier. Europe now knew that America would fight to protect her interests. It was, therefore, no accident that differences with Britain were settled with swiftness and dispatch. In 1817 both she and the United States agreed to a limitation of armaments upon the Great Lakes. A year later, after intensive negotiations, they settled upon a boundary which ran along the 49th parallel from the Lake of the Woods to the Rocky Mountains and which left the Oregon Territory open to citizens of both nations. They also resolved the nagging problem of the fisheries by granting to the United States the perpetual liberty to fish along specified portions of the coasts of Labrador and Newfoundland as well as the right to cure fish on more limited sections of the unsettled shores of these two territories. It was not long after this that America secured the rest of Florida. And in 1823 the President enunciated the Monroe Doctrine. America had freed herself from Europe, and decades were to pass before she was again to become seriously involved with the great powers of that continent.

During this time she was able to devote her energies and talents to building a nation which stretched from the Atlantic to the Pacific and from the Gulf of Mexico to the Canadian border. It was never to extend above the Canadian border, however, for the war had created a profound distrust of American intentions in Canada and an unshakeable determination

---

[33] Gallatin to Lyon, May 7, 1816, Henry Adams, *The Writings of Albert Gallatin* (3 vols., Philadelphia, 1879), I, 700.

among her people to preserve their own identity. But if the United States found expansion to the north closed, the swiftness of her expansion westward was an accomplishment of enormous magnitude. The ease and rapidity of this movement westward was the result in some measure, of the war, for one of its unexpected and important consequences was the growth of the American economy. Cut off from British supplies on which she had depended for so long, the United States was forced to develop and diversify her own industries. As Jefferson said, "We owe to their [Britain's] past follies and wrongs the incalculable advantage of being made independent of them for every material manufacture. These have taken such root, in our private families especially, that nothing can now extirpate them." [34] This new economic strength added to the new freedom from the Old World provided the United States with an impetus for growth that might otherwise not have existed. This was answer enough to those critics who argued that the war need never have been fought.

------

[34] Jefferson to Crawford, Feb. 11, 1815, Lipscomb and Bergh (eds.), *The Writings of Thomas Jefferson*, XIV, 244.

Suggestions for Further Reading

THE COMING OF THE WAR

For many years after it was fought, the War of 1812 was either ignored or treated cursorily by historians. However, in recent years a number of excellent studies of this difficult conflict have appeared. The classic accounts of the war were written either at the end of the last century or the beginning of this one. Henry Adams, *History of the United States of America during the Administrations of Jefferson and Madison* (9 vols., New York, 1891) and A. T. Mahan, *Sea Power in its Relation to the War of 1812* (2 vols., London, 1905), both emphasized maritime disputes as a cause of the war. J. W. Pratt, *Expansionists of 1812* (New York, 1925), stressed the role of the West in bringing on the conflict. A. L. Burt, *The United States, Great Britain and British North America from the Revolution to the Establishment of Peace after the War of 1812* (New Haven, 1940) in a wise and judicious study of the period emphasized again the importance of maritime issues. W. H. Goodman, "The Origins of the War of 1812: A Survey of Changing Interpretations," *Mississippi Valley Historical Review*, XXVIII (1941), 171–186, gave a valuable synthesis of views concerning the origins of the war. The effects of British maritime policies upon the economy of the South and the West were studied in G. R. Taylor, "Agrarian Discontent in the Mississippi Valley Preceding the War of 1812," *Journal of Political Economy*, XXXIX (1931), 471–505, and Margaret K. Latimer, "South Carolina—A Protagonist of the War of 1812," *American Historical Review*, LXI (1956), 914–929. See also Abbot Smith, "Mr. Madison's War: An Unsuccessful Experiment in the Conduct of National Policy," *Political Science Quarterly*, LVII (1942), 229–246. Bradford Perkins, *Prologue to War* (Berkeley, 1961), a recent work of extensive research, stressed the complicated nature of the origins of the war and emphasized the importance of maritime issues in precipitating it. Reginald Horsman, *The Causes of the War of 1812* (Philadelphia, 1962), gave a compact analysis of the coming of the war that also emphasized the European origins of the disputes drawing the United States into war. Irving Brant, *James Madison: the President, 1809–1812* (Indianapolis, 1956), attempted, not with complete success, to raise Madison's stature as a political leader. Roger Brown, *The Republic in Peril: 1812* (New York, 1964), argued that party allegiance rather than sectional interests explained the divisions of opinion that distracted the country and Congress before the declaration of war. N. K. Risjord, "1812: Conservatives, War Hawks, and the Nation's Honor," *William and Mary Quarterly*, XVIII (1961), 196–210, suggested that the desire to preserve national honor was the driving force behind the War Hawks' determination to fight Britain. Bernard Mayo, *Henry Clay* (Boston, 1937), is an excellent biography of one of the war's leading advocates. A. Z. Carr, *The Coming of the War* (Garden City, New York, 1960), is a general account of the coming of the war. Specific material on the importance and the effects of the embargo may be found in L. M. Sears, *Jefferson and the Embargo* (Durham, 1927) and Leonard White, *The Jeffersonians—A Study in Administrative History, 1801–1829* (New York, 1951). Detailed treatment of maritime disputes may be examined in J. F. Zimmerman, *Impressment of American Seamen* (New York, 1925), W. H. Phillips and A. H. Reede, *Neutrality* (New York, 1936), and E. Hecksher, *The Continental System* (Oxford, 1922). Information on particular problems is to be found in Reginald Horsman, "Western War Aims, 1811–1812," *Indiana Magazine of History*, LIII (1957), 1–18, and "British Indian Policy in the Northwest, 1807–1812," *Mississippi Valley Historical Review*, XLV (1958), 51–66; Bradford Perkins, "George Canning, Great Britain, and the United States, 1807–1809," *American Historical Review*, LXIII (1957), 1–22; A. Steel, "Impressment in the Monroe-Pinkney Negotiations, 1806–1807," *American Historical Review*, LVII (1952), 352–369; and L. M. Hacker, "Western Land Hunger and the War of 1812," *Mississippi Valley Historical Review*, X (1924), 365–395.

MILITARY AND NAVAL OPERATIONS

The most extensive study of wartime operations is to be found in A. T. Mahan, *Sea Power in its Relation to the War of 1812* (2 vols., London, 1905). An excellent collection of articles dealing with operations on the Canadian border has recently been published in Morris Zaslow (ed.), *The Defended Border: Upper Canada and The War of 1812* (Toronto, 1964). Further information may be found in Sir Charles P. Lucas, *The Canadian War of 1812* (Oxford, 1906). For an American treatment, see F. F. Beirne, *The War of 1812* (New York, 1949).

THE MAKING OF PEACE

The most detailed treatment of the peace negotiations is in F. A. Updyke, *The Diplomacy of the War of 1812* (Baltimore, 1915). The most recent study of the negotiations is Bradford Perkins, *Castlereagh and Adams* (Berkeley, 1964). Additional information may be studied in S. F. Bemis, *John Quincy Adams and the Foundation of American Foreign Policy* (New York, 1949); Irving Brant, *James Madison: Commander in Chief, 1812–1836* (Indianapolis, 1961); F. L. Engelman, *The Peace of Christmas Eve* (New York, 1962); Raymond Walters, Jr., *Albert Gallatin: Jeffersonian Financier and Diplomat* (New York, 1957); and W. D. Jones, "A British View of the War of 1812 and the Peace Negotiations," *Mississippi Valley Historical Review*, XLV, 1958, 481–487.

Index